ASTROLOGICAL TREATISES

by MÂSHÂ·ALLÂH

Translated from the Latin

by

James Herschel Holden, M.A.
Fellow of the American Federation of Astrologers

ISBN-10: 0-86690-598-7
ISBN-13: 978-0-86690-598-5

First Printing 2009

Cover Design: Jack Cipolla

Published by:
American Federation of Astrologers, Inc.
6535 S. Rural Road
Tempe, AZ 85283

www.astrologers.com

Printed in the United States of America.

TABLE OF CONTENTS

PREFACE TO
ASTROLOGICAL TREATISES
by MÂSHÂ>ALLÂH

This volume contains several astrological treatises by Mâshâ>allâh translated from the Latin versions into English. The first is *The Book of Reception in Horary Questions*. This book sets forth a system of interpretation of Horary charts that relies heavily on reception of the rulers.

The second treatise is *The Book of Natitivities*. It is based upon the method of interpretation set forth by Dorotheus of Sidon (1st century), which made use of the Ruler of the ASC, the Light of the Time and its ruler, and the rulers of their Triplicities, as well as the Hyleg and the *Alcochoden*.

The third treatise is *The Book on the Revolutions of Years*. This is a treatise on Mundane Astrology with special reference to Aries Ingresses as they are called today.

The fourth treatise is *The Book of the Significations of the Planets in Nativities*. It gives the significations of the Planets in their own domiciles and in the domiciles of the other Planets. Then it gives the significations of the ruler of each House when it is located in each of the twelve Houses. And finally, the Significations of the Planets when they are located in their own terms or in those of the other Planets.

The fifth treatise is *The Epistle on Conjunctions*. It is a short treatise on astrometeorology with special reference to the Conjunctions of the Outer Planets.

The sixth treatise is *The Book of Thoughts and Intentions.*

Each of these treatises has its own Title Page, Preface, Text, Index of Persons, and Bibliography. Personal information about the astrologer Mâshâʾallâh is given most fully in the Preface to *The Book of Reception in Horary Questions*.

Here it will be sufficient to say that Mâshâʾallâh was one of the earliest astrologers to write books on astrology in the Arabic language.[1] By the later writers in Arabic he was considered to be a prime astrological authority. And his fame endured among the European astrologers who read the numerous astrological treatises translated into Latin in the 12th century. In particular, he was often mentioned by the 13th century writers Guido Bonatti and Leopold of Austria.

---

[1]Perhaps the earliest was Theophilus of Edessa (8th century), but he never received the acclaim that Mâshâʾallâh received, and his books were not translated into Latin, so he has remained largely unknown to Western astrologers.

MÂSHÂ>ALLÂH

THE BOOK OF RECEPTION
IN HORARY QUESTIONS

Translated from the Twelfth Century Latin Version
of John of Seville

by

JAMES HERSCHEL HOLDEN, M.A.
Fellow of the American Federation of Astrologers

Contents

Translator's Preface

Mâshâ'allâh was the adopted Muslim name of the Jewish astrologer Mîshâ ibn Athrâ from Basra, Iraq, who converted to Islam and became one of the greatest Arabian[1] astrologers. He was born about 730 A.D. and lived until about 815. He was one of the astrological consultants employed by the Caliph al-Manṣûr (c.712-777) to make an election for the founding of the new city of Baghdad in 762.[2] Al-Nadîm[3] says this about Mâshâ'allâh: "He was a man of distinction and during his period the leading person for the science of judgments of the stars." He was the author of twenty or more books, one of them on the astrolabe. Several of his books were translated into Latin in the 12th century.

In *The Book of Reception in Horary Questions*, the reader will be struck by the frequent references to God's will. As a convert to Islam, Mâshâ'allâh was careful to proclaim his orthodoxy in the matter of fate. Muslim theology proclaims that God (Allâh) directs the lives of humans from birth to death. So an astrologer had to be careful not to ascribe a particular life event solely to the stars. Hence, the frequent addition of the phrase, "by the will of God."

Mâshâ'allâh was probably acquainted with the Greek astrologer Theophilus of Edessa (d.777), who seems to have been the first

---

[1] By *Arabian astrologers*, I mean all those, of whatever ethnic group, who wrote in the Arabic language.

[2] See my paper "The Foundation Chart of Baghdad" in *Today's Astrologer* Vol. 65, No. 3 (March 2, 2003): 9-10 & 29.

[3] See the priceless catalogue of Arabic literature as it existed at the end of the 10th century, *The Fihrist of al-Nadîm* edited and translated by Bayard Dodge (New York and London: Columbia Univerity Press, 1970. 2 vols.), II, p. 650.

prominent "Arabian" astrologer. Theophilus wrote several books on astrology that still survive in Greek versions,[1] but the Arabic versions were unknown to the Twelfth Century Translators, who turned much Arabian astrology into Latin and sparked the recovery of astrology in Western Europe.

Mâshâʾallâh thus became the earliest Arabian astrologer whose works were known in the West. He wrote on a variety of subjects and was considered by both later Arabian astrologers and European astrologers to be a prime authority. His book on *Reception in Horary Astrology* was translated into Latin by John of Seville in 1148 as *De receptione in interrogationibus* 'On Reception in Horary Questions'. It is especially interesting because it contains five example Horary charts from his own private practice in the 790s under the Caliph Hârûn al-Rashîd (ruled 786-809). These are thus some of the earliest Horary charts available for study.[2]

The first edition of this book was published in 1484 by Erhard Ratdolt at Venice in an omnibus edition of astrological works. I have used a xerox copy of the Latin text included in the omnibus edition published at Venice by Bonetus Locatellus in 1493. The text is neatly printed in two columns of abbreviated Latin on folios 143^r-148^r. The charts are of course in the old square format, but I have redrawn them in the modern round format for the convenience of the reader.

The term *reception* refers to the position of a Planet in a sign that is ruled by another Planet, e.g. Saturn in Taurus; since Saturn is in a sign ruled by Venus; it is said to be *received* by Venus; and Venus is also said to be its *dispositor*. Reception can also occur when a Planet is in the exaltation sign of another Planet, e.g. Saturn in Pisces could be said to be *received* by Venus, because Pisces is the exaltation sign of Venus. Mâshâʾallâh says that a consideration of reception is of fundamental importance in interpreting a

---

[1]David Pingree edited some of the Greek versions, but they have never been published.

[2]The charts are included in O. Neugebauer and H. B. Van Hoesen, *Greek Horoscopes* (Philadelphia: The American Philosophical Society, 1959).

Horary chart. Another technique that Mâshâ⁾allâh makes constant use of is considering the configurations when the Moon or a Planet moves into the next sign from where it is at the moment of the Question. He explains both of these techniques in great detail, illustrating them with actual example charts.

We can see from the charts that Mâshâ⁾allâh did not use the tropical zodiac. He used some tables that were based upon a fixed zodiac. These tables seem to have been the *Zîj al-Shâh* or 'Tables of the King'. In the late 8th century their fixed zodiac differed from the tropical zodiac by about 4.5 degrees. For comparison, I have used positions calculated from my computerized version of the old Hindu *Surya Siddhanta* Tables. These are older tables than those of the Zîj al-Shâh, but they yield Sun and Moon positions that are fairly close to the positions in Mâshâ⁾allâh's charts, and the planetary positions are usually within a few degrees.

If the reader wants to recalculate the charts, he should remember that the ASC and MC degrees, like the Planets' places are referred to a fixed zodiac, so that the longitudes are about 4.5 degrees less than those in the tropical zodiac. In giving times for which the charts were calculated by Mâshâ⁾allâh, I have assumed that he would have reckoned the time to be the nearest hour, quarter hour, or half hour.

The system of house division used by Mâshâ⁾allâh is not stated explicitly, but since in several places he refers to the signs as houses, it would appear that he used either the Sign-House system or the Equal House system. However, he does mention the degree of the MC in his statements of the chart positions, so he may have been using the Alchabitius system. And he also sometimes mentions intermediate house cusps with the variation set forth by Ptolemy, so that might indicate his use of the Equal House system (or else, of his adaptation of Ptolemy's rule to the cusps of the Alchabitius system).

The intermediate house cusps of the charts in the printed book were not mentioned by Mâshâ⁾allâh, so they were probably determined by the editor of the 1493 edition, and they may have been intended to be either Porphyry or Alchabitius cusps, but if so, they were poorly calculated. However, I have shown them on the charts just as they appear in the 1493 edition. The reader can ignore them or substitute those of his own choice.

In translating the Latin into English, I have generally adhered to the technical terms employed by the great modern master William Lilly. For example, the person asking the Question is the *Querent*, and what he asks about is the thing *Quesited,* or more commonly simply the *thing*. If the Querent wants to know whether a certain event will occur or whether he will obtain something that he desires, then the chart is studied by the rules to determine whether the thing inquired about will or will not occur or be obtained, and the technical terms for this determination are *perfection* and *non-perfection*.

The Planets are divided into two groups that are called *fortuni* and *mali* in Latin, i.e. *fortunes* and *infortunes*, but I have chosen to translate them as *benefics* and *malefics*. And I have preferred the older term *evil* as the translation for the Latin word *malum*. The very frequent term *conjunctio* 'conjunction' usually means 'connection', i.e. by either a physical conjunction or by an aspect. If it appears to refer to an actual conjunction, I have translated it as 'conjunction'; but more often it appears to refer to an aspect, in which case I have translated it as 'connection'. This Latin text uses the singular *terminum* 'term' for the five-fold subdivisions of the signs, but I have translated it by the plural 'terms', since in classical Greek and Latin astrological texts it means 'boundaries' and is therefore plural. And I have translated *ascendens* 'ascendant' as ASC and *medium caeli* 'middle of heaven' as MC.

Paragraphing and punctuation were still primitive in the 15th century. The Latin text of the 1493 edition has few intermediate paragraphs and only the period and the colon. I have modernized it by arbitrarily breaking the solid text into paragraphs, and by inserting commas, semicolons, and dashes. Consequently, some Latin sentences that were divided in the 1493 edition are joined together in the translation, and some excessively long sentences have been broken up into shorter ones. These actions are necessary when dealing with medieval texts; consequently, modern editions and translations differ in their presentation of the text.

James H. Holden
27 October 2007

THE BOOK OF RECEPTION IN
HORARY QUESTIONS

A certain man of the learned men brought forth a book of the books of the secrets of the stars from those that the kings treasured, and he disclosed its intention in all those things that men need in their own things about interrogations. And it was from it that he brought forth and disclosed in the things of interrogations whether a thing is to be or not to be, and when it will be if it should be done; and when there shall appear that which is not, if it should not be done; and what will prohibit it if it is not [done], and through whom it is done, and whence it should be done.

And the knowledge of this thing, and its explanation is in the 7 Planets and in their 12 domiciles, and in the 7 exaltations of the Planets, and in their falls, and in their connections[1]; also, in their separations and in their mutual receptions, and in the return of reception, and in the mutual giving[2] of their disposition. And the significator will be the one to which the disposition comes, by the will of God; which, if it is in the condition of the effecting of the thing, it will signify its effecting; and if it is in the state of prohibition, it will signify its prohibition, by the will of God.

---

[1]Here and very frequently below., the Latin has the word *coniunctio* 'conjunction', but it more often means 'connection by aspect' rather than 'conjunction by body', so I have tried to restrict 'conjunction' in the translation to the instances where 'conjunction by body' seems to be meant.

[2]The Latin text has *pulsatione* 'striking', but this is a common mistranslation of the Arabic verb *dafaʿa,* which can mean 'striking', but also 'giving'. Here it should be translated as *donatione* 'giving'.

The Reception and Connection of the Planets.

Know that reception is made by exaltations and domiciles; however, in the cause of things whether they are or not; that is, as there is some Planet of the 7 in the exaltations of another Planet, or in its domicile; and that one is joined to it by known aspects[1]; or both of them are in one sign, and one of them, i.e. one of the 7, is joined to it in the exaltation of its companion; then it is joined to it by its own body.

Of which thing, this is an example: let Saturn be in Aries in the 20th degree and Mars in the 15th degree of that same Aries; then Mars is joined to Saturn by its own body, and Mars receives Saturn in its own domicile; but Saturn does not receive Mars; this is done when there is not any Planet in known aspects that is near to the connection of Saturn by degree, that is by a degree before Mars. But if there is in the known aspects or in Aries a Planet that is closer to the connection of Saturn, that one will be more worthy of the connection of Saturn than Mars is; for the true conjunction is by one degree upon another[2] of the conjunction rather than by aspect.

Another example of connection and reception is when Saturn is in Aries in the 20th degree and Mars is in Capricorn in the 10th degree; and none of the planets is closer than Mars to the connection of Saturn by one degree on another; then they receive each other mutually by domiciles; for Mars receives Saturn because it is in its own domicile; and Saturn receives Mars because it is in its own domicile; similarly too, exaltations are just like domiciles; but exaltations are of greater authority in ruling; namely, if the Question is about a King; the ruler of an exaltation is stronger than the ruler of a domicile.

Therefore, when the Sun is in Aries in the 10th degree, and Mars is in Capricorn in the 10th degree, the Sun is then joined to Mars,

---

[1]The known aspects are the sextile, square, trine, and opposition. (The conjunction is not an *aspect* but rather a *position*.)

[2]By "one degree upon another," he refers to a partile conjunction or aspect, where the degree numbers are the same.

and Mars receives the Sun because it is in the domicile of Mars; but the Sun does not receive Mars because it is not in the Sun's domicile.

Similarly, with the rest of the 7 Planets; and whichever one of them is joined to its own companion by its own domicile or exaltation, by known aspects, or is in the same sign; it will project and commit to it its own disposition, if the former one receives the one to which it commits; it perfects its own thing by the will of God. And the Sun in that aspect does not receive Mars because it is not in its domicile nor in its own exaltation, and Mars does receive the Sun which is in its own domicile.

And if the Sun is in Libra in the 1st degree, and Saturn is in Aries in the 25th degree, and no Planet is in Aries nor in any aspects closer than the Sun to the connection of Saturn; and Saturn does not go out of Aries until the Sun is joined to it partilely, the Sun receives Saturn, and Saturn receives the Sun, for each one of them receives its own companion, in this case by exaltation; and if it is in opposition or square aspect, it signifies error, labor, anxiety, and contrariety; and if it is in connection by trine aspect or sextile, it signifies lightness and directness.

And when the Sun is joined to Saturn, and Saturn receives the Sun, and it is received by the Sun by domicile namely or by exaltation, they will be at peace, and the cause will be perfected by the will of God.

Similarly, [in the case of] all the Planets, benefics with benefics increase good, and malefics with malefics are made good on account of reception; that is, they make good, and their evil and impediment goes away. And benefics with malefics are at peace and their evil goes away, and they perfect [the thing], unless by square aspect or by opposition, because there is some labor and error in that.

But if it is the Sun in Aries and Saturn in Libra, just as I have already said to you about a connection, there will be enmities and contrarieties and misunderstandings and denials; and one of these does not receive its companion; and all the Planets act similarly, for the connection is by the opposition of the known aspects, i.e. by trine and square and sextile aspect, and by conjunction; and this is done in known domiciles; and whatever is between two signs is separated from a conjunction, that is when a Planet enters a second sign before there is joined to it a Planet that is going to it, but is not [yet] joined to it.

And know that a connection is in this manner—whichever one of the 7 Planets, namely a light one, is joined to a heavy one—and a heavy one is not joined to a light one, because a light one comes next to a heavy one, and the heavy one does not come next to the light one; for a connection is also partilely; then it is joined to it and it commits its own disposition to it; and after that it is separated from it, and it does not leave off aspecting the one with which it was joined, until it is separated from it.

But the connection is an aspect, because whenever there is a Planet going to a Planet in its own light and its own nature, it will be aspecting it until it projects its own light upon it partilely; then it will be a true connection, and it will commit its own thing to it; after that, it is separated from it, and it is the end of that aspect; in this manner the Planet will indicate that which is not yet; when it is going to the connection; and when it is separated from it, it will indicate that which will transpire and what has already been done; namely, it will indicate from the star from which it is separated what has already occurred; and it indicates from the star to which it is joined what will be.

Questions of the ASC.

And first about any particular thing, whether it will be perfected or not; and about any rumor, whether it is true or not.

When, therefore, you have been asked about any particular thing, whether it will be perfected or not; or about any rumor, whether it may be true or not; you will take the shadow of the gnomon,[1] the same namely in the hour in which there comes forth the word from the mouth of the one asking about the thing; and if it is a man who is asking for himself, or if it is a letter written by his own hand; but if he does not know how to write, he sends to you such a one who is anxious about his own thing; and you do not ask of him anything about it, until you understand it; and this should not be unless it is about the thing concerning which there is great anxiety, or about a truly necessary thing; and it does not suit a wise man to look for himself, but he ought to ask another.[2]

And when the sign of the ASC and its degree has become known to you, and the sign of the MC and its degree,[3] and you have noted the dispositors of the 7 Planets, by the will of God, in their own degrees in the domiciles in which they are, and in their own minutes with a very certain and correct number, from which there is nothing more or less,[4] then look at the ruler of the ASC and the Moon; and whichever one of them you find to be stronger, work with it and let the other be its partner.

That is, you will begin to inspect the ruler of the ASC, which if it aspects the sign of the ASC, this will be its strong testimony to work through it; and the Moon will work in partnership with it from whatever place it is in. And if the ruler of the ASC does not aspect the ASC, look to see whether it is joined to a Planet that does aspect the sign of the ASC from its own place and returns its own light to the ASC itself, or is joined to a Planet that is cadent from the ASC, and that cadent planet is joined to another one aspecting the sign of the ASC, which elevates it and returns its light to the ascending sign.

But if the ruler of the ASC is joined to a Planet aspecting the sign of the ASC, or the same ruler of the ASC is joined to a Planet,

---

[1]That is, by day take the time from the shadow on the sun dial.

[2]That is, a skilled astrologer should not try to interpret a Horary chart for a personal Question, but he should ask another astrologer to interpret it for him.

[3]This implies that Mâshâ'allâh used a quadrant system of house division—probably the Alchabitius system. But elsewhere he seems to be referring to charts drawn in the Sign-House system.

[4]He refers to an accurately calculated chart.

and that Planet is joined to another one that returns its own light to the sign of the ASC, it will elevate it. And if there is a connection from one Planet to another of the 7 Planets, there will be the same work in them. One of them, namely, will elevate the light of the first one to the other one, until it comes to the last of them.

But if the ruler of the ASC gives[1] its own light to the sign of the ASC, work through it, and the Moon participates in this. And if the ruler of the ASC sign does not aspect the ASC, and it is not joined to a Planet that is aspecting the ASC and returning and giving[2] its light to it, because having given its aspect to the ASC, its outcome is when it does not aspect, nor does it return the light of the planet aspecting the ASC. But if the ruler of the ASC does not aspect the ASC, then it is impedited and evil.

Then [it is necessary] to work through the Moon, just as you work through the ruler of the ASC. And know that according to the quantity of the impediment that entered upon it, i.e. upon the ruler of the ASC, it will then therefore be necessary to work by the Moon, which if it aspects the ASC, or if any one of the Planets returns its light to the ASC, it will be necessary to work through it; and the ruler of the ASC will participate in it.

Look at the Moon, which if it aspects the sign ascending, [it will be necessary] to work through it, and the ruler of the ASC will participate in it by the same condition, namely if the ruler of the ASC does not aspect the ASC, and it is not joined to any Planet that returns its own light to the ASC; [then] see to which of the 7 Planets the Moon is then joined, and work through that one; and the ruler of the ASC will participate with it.

And if the Moon does not aspect the ASC and is not joined to any Planet that returns its own light to the ASC, or if the Moon is aspecting the ASC and is not conjoined to any Planet—that is, if it is *void of course*—and the ruler of the ASC does not aspect the

---

[1]Again, the Latin text has *pulsat* 'strikes' where it should have *donat* 'gives'.

[2]Here too, reading *donanti* 'giving' instead of *pulsanti* 'striking'. Changed hereafter without notice.

ASC, and it is also *void of course*, then look at which one of them must more quickly leave the sign in which it is, and which one has less degrees, i.e. which one has fewer degrees to go out of, and you will change that one to the sign that is next from its own place.[1]

After that, you will look at which one of the planets it is joined to first, and judge by that one. And all the Planets are changed; but the lighter Planet is the more worthy of change than the more weighty one, because of course the weakening of the Planets indicates worthlessness, i.e. the evil of the thing and its slowness; and every Planet with the worthlessness of its own course indicates much slowness; also the few number of degrees of a Planet, which should perambulate in the sign in which it is; and much slowness after the Question indicates the slowness or quickness of the effect of the thing; the one therefore that exits quicker from the sign in which it is will be quicker in [effecting] the thing. But the light and heavy [Planet], when it is *void of course* indicates the slowness of things and their worthlessness.

Therefore, when you find the ruler of the ASC and the Moon *void of course*, joining themselves to no [Planet], it pronounces the slowness of the thing and its prolongation, and that it must be postponed according to what you see. And see to which [Planet] the Moon is joined on its first coming out of the sign in which it is; and judge the effect of that thing by the will of God; and the ruler of the ASC will participate in it according to its strength or debility in the place in which it is.

There will also participate with them in the work a Planet that is in the ASC, as well as a Planet that is in the house of the thing quesited, which, if it is a partner to the sign in which it is, and it is received, it indicates the goodness of the thing and its worthiness; and if it is not a partner to the same sign in which it is, and it is not received, it indicates the impediment of that same thing and its worthlessness. Moreover, the effecting of the thing and its prohibition is not from that one that is in the ASC, but it is made on the

---

[1]That is, you interpret it as if it were in the next sign.

part of the ruler of the ASC or the Moon, and from the stars to which they are joined and their connection and reception, and from the return of their reception.

And know that the Moon is a partner of the ruler of the ASC always in the same place, by the will of God. Therefore, when you find the ruler of the ASC impedited, [it is necessary] to work through the Moon, just as you work through the ruler of the ASC.

A Question about the Death or Life of the Querent in the Year of his Question.

But if you have looked for a man who has asked you about his life—namely, whether he might die in that year or not—you will look for him just as you would look for a sick person. Look at the one to which the ruler of the ASC is joined; but if the ruler of the ASC is joined to a benefic Planet, and that benefic is the dispositor to which the disposition comes, and it does not return it to another, and that benefic is not the ruler of the House of Death, say that he will not die in that same year, by the will of God.

And if the ruler of the ASC is conjoined to an evil Planet or to the ruler of the House of Death, whatever kind it is—either a malefic or a benefic—and the ruler of the ASC itself is not received, and that malefic Planets do not receive it, nor does the ruler of the House of Death, malefic or benefic, [then] look at the Moon—if she is also evil, he will die by the will of God in that same year.

Then look at when the ruler of the ASC may be joined to that evil Planet or to the ruler of the House of Death that does not receive it partilely, and put that for the [number of] days. But if it is not then, it will be when it comes to it by its own body, and when it has come to its degree and is conjoined to it partilely by its own body; then he will die.

But if the ruler of the ASC is joined to a Planet that does not receive it, then the sick person or the Querent will escape death in that same year, by the will of God; and the sick person will recover from his sickness, by the will of God.

And if the ruler of the ASC is impedited, [it is necessary] to work with the Moon, just as I have already told you about the ruler of the ASC; and judge by it, just as you have judged by the ruler of the ASC.

As for [whether] good fortune and health will be bestowed on him by his sickness, look at when the ruler of the ASC will be joined to the planet that signified his health partilely, and put those days as degrees, namely of the connection; but if it is not then, it will be when it is joined to it by its own body in the sign in which it is, or when it is joined to it in another place or in one of the angles. If it is already removed from it, then he will escape [harm], if God wills.

But if the ruler of the ASC is joined to the ruler of the House of Death, or if the ruler of the House of Death is joined to it, he will die, by the will of God; and the Moon should not be considered in this case. And if the ruler of the ASC is strong and not impedited, and the Moon is joined to the ruler of the House of Death, he will be freed, by the will of God, because the ruler of the House of the Ascendant rules more by itself in life and in death than the Moon does; and the Moon participates with it in everything.

And here I am putting for you a Question about this—namely, about a sick person, whether he would be freed from his sickness, or whether he would die, by the will of God.

The Question, of which the sign Virgo was ascending the 15th degree, and the MC was the 15th degree of Gemini; and Mars was in Gemini in 15 degrees and 30 minutes, and the Moon in Taurus in 26 degrees and 25 minutes, and Jupiter in Taurus in 19 degrees and 15 minutes, and the Sun in 20 degrees and 30 minutes of Aries, and Saturn in Aries in 10 degrees and 15 minutes, and Mercury in Aries in 24 degrees and 50 minutes, and Venus in Pisces in the 5th degree and 37 minutes, as is shown in this figure. [1]

---

[1] The figure was presumably set for Baghdad at about 3:30 PM LAT (=3:12 PM LMT) on Monday 11 April 791. The planetary positions were calculated from tables based on a fixed zodiac. *Surya Siddhanta* positions would agree closely for the Sun, Moon, and Saturn, and would be within a few degrees for the others. It is

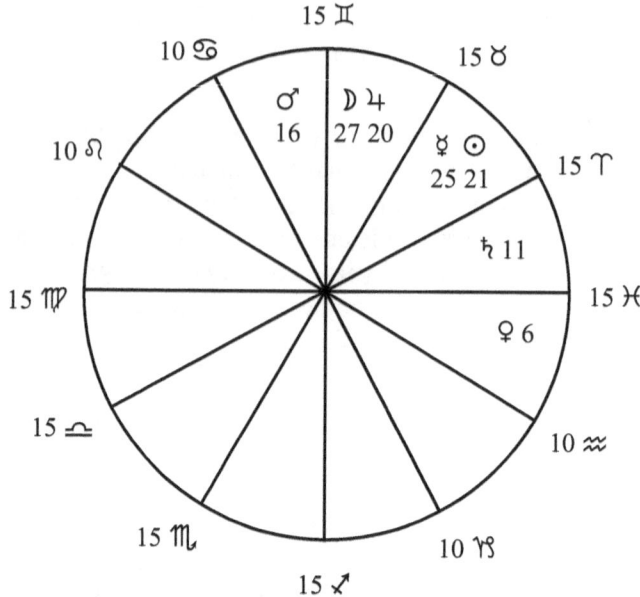

By the will of God, I looked at the ASC of this Question, and its ruler, and the Moon, and the rest of the seven [Planets], and the angles. And the ruler of the ASC was *void of course* in the House of Death; it was [therefore] signifying the strength of pain and the fear of death. And Mars was the ruler of the House of Death, in the MC aspecting the House of Life, also signifying the strength of his pain and the loss of hope.

After that, I looked at the Moon, whom I also found to be *void of course*, but it was aspecting the House of Life from the 9th house; and the Moon was stronger in signification than the ruler of the ASC, because she was aspecting the sign of the ASC, and she was

---

uncertain what system of house division Mâshâ'allâh used. I have shown the cuspal numbers from the chart in the printed book. They are approximately Alchabitius cusps (their true values would be about 13 Cancer and 13 Leo for XI and XII and 17 Libra and 17 Scorpio for II and III). For the convenience of the reader, I have drawn the chart in the modern round form.

swifter, i.e. she would be the first to move out of the sign in which she was. They therefore signified by their being *void of course* a prolongation of the sickness and the severity of it.

And I changed the Moon from the sign in which it was, because that Planet had gone through the degrees in its own sign [before] Mercury. And Mercury will have left more swiftly from the sign in which it was; and it was stronger because it would aspect the ascending sign and it would receive it. And it is joined to Venus at its own first connection, giving, i.e. committing its own disposition to it. And Venus was joined to Jupiter and was receiving him, and they were receiving each other by domiciles and by connection; and it was Jupiter when the disposition came to him, not committing his own disposition to another, because it was not being joined to Saturn, which is heavier than all the Planets, and Jupiter is joined to none of the Planets except it.

It signified, therefore, that when Jupiter came to it, the disposition from Venus which committed her to it was receiving it; and it was being received by him by domiciles and by connection, the sick person would come into health and good fortune. But his sickness would be on the increase until Venus would be joined to Jupiter partilely; and when Venus would be separated from Jupiter by one minute, the sickness would begin to be diminished, by the will of God, [and] health and freedom [from pain] would come.

[And if] the ruler of this Question had [not] been just as we said previously, his pain would not have ceased to increase, nor would his fear of death, until Venus was joined partilely to Jupiter. Therefore, when Venus would have separated from Jupiter, health and quiet and [a condition of] little pain would have begun. It is by the will of God.

And if the connection had come to Mars, i.e. if Venus would have been joined to Mars, which was the ruler of the house of Death, in place of Jupiter, and he would not have received her, it could be said that he would die by the will of God when Venus would be joined to Mars and would project her rays onto him, and

[also] her light, which is the true connection, because Mars is the ruler of the House of Death, which is the thing about which the Querent is asking.

And so, when the ruler of the ASC is always joined to the ruler of the thing quesited of all [possible] things, the thing about which the Question is put is done, by the will of God, because death is not like other things. And when [the Question] is [about] death, it should not be looked at what might be afterwards, just as would be done in the case of the rest of things [that might be asked], because when the ruler of the ASC and the Moon are joined to the ruler of the thing, they say that the thing will be; [and] after that, the ruler of the house of the thing is looked at [to see] to what [Planet] it commits its own disposition after its effecting. Which, if it is a benefic, they say that the thing will be made better. And if it is a malefic, they say that the thing will be subsequently destroyed.

Moreover, when you look at [a Question of] death, and you find the ruler of the ASC and the Moon joined to the ruler of the House of Death, the sick person will be dead of that sickness, by the will of God, unless the ruler of the House of Death, which is the ruler of the same thing, receives them. And know that if the ruler of the House of Death is joined to the ruler of the ASC, you will also judge similarly that he is going to die of his sickness, by the will of God.

And know that Venus, to whom the Moon is joined, if she were joined to the Sun, and if the Sun would be the ruler of the House of Life, and if he would be joined to Jupiter by [one of] the known aspects that is weaker, or by his own body which is stronger; [and] if there was not a strong reception between them, and if the Sun was not impeded by Jupiter in that figure, because it is the ruler of the house of the thing quesited, and Venus is joined to the Sun, and the Sun is joined to Jupiter, and Jupiter is a benefic, and the Sun is a benefic, and the Moon was joined to Venus, and Venus was joined to the Sun, and the Sun was joined to Jupiter. The Sun, therefore, signified the outcome of life, and it is its significator, and it carried its light to Jupiter, which is the *Almuten*,[1] that is [the Planet] that has the rulership in this figure; and it was life for him, and it did not destroy him, because the benefics also have the nature of life, unless they are those benefics that are rulers of the House of Death.

But then, the Sun destroys the stars by combustion when it does not receive them by a strong reception by domiciles, namely, and by exaltations; and if the stars were already cadent in combustion and by conjunction; or if the Sun projects his own light onto the stars by known aspects, namely by square and opposition, and without strong reception, and it is not the ruler of the ASC.

And when it would impedite any Planet which is closer than the rest [of the Planets] in conjunction or aspect, and it is not in one degree, it destroys him, and all the work that it rules, by the will of God, whether it is a malefic or a benefic; if the Sun is not the ruler of the House of Life, it will destroy him too, unless it receives it.

And know that when a Planet is in the House of Death and is a malefic, and the ruler of the ASC is joined to it, or when it is a benefic and it has a dignity in the House of Death; and between it and the ruler of the ASC there is no reception, it will also signify death. And the conjunction of the ruler of the House of Death with a planet that is in the House of Life, [will act] similarly.

It also signifies the diversity of the condition of the sick person., namely health and sickness, a multitude of connections of the planets, and the diversity of their natures in good or evil; and reception and non-reception, because when the ruler of the ASC or the Moon is joined to a benefic or a malefic that receives it, the condition of the sick person will not cease until it commits its own disposition to him partilely; then, if that Planet to which the Moon or the ruler of the ASC commits[its own disposition] is joined to no [Planet], the sick [person] will be freed from his sickness], and his health will be improved; and if that Planet commits its own disposition to a malefic that does not receive it, or to a benefic not re-

---

[1]The Latin text has *alimbutar*, which appears to be a corruption of *al-mubtazz*, the *Almuten*.

ceiving it, which is the ruler of the House of Death, and the disposition is its own and not that of another, i.e. it commits its disposition to it and not to another, he will die.

If the ruler of the ASC or the Moon is separated from that Planet that receives it; and that Planet commits its own disposition to a malefic Planet that does not receive it, or to a benefic that does not receive it, which is the ruler of the House of Death, the sick person will be broken down, i.e. he will be sickened and returned to his own sickness. And when that Planet is conjoined to the same malefic partilely, he will die by the will of God. And if it is received, his sickness will be prolonged until its disposition comes to that same Planet; after that, he will be freed [from his sickness], by the will of God.

Therefore, look at the planet to which the connection comes, because it is the ruler of its thing, and it rules it by the will of God; and the beneficence of the Planets and their malice or impediment, also of their receivers and non-reception, will indicate to you the lightness of the thing or its weight,[1] also its effecting and its prohibition; but the end of the thing will be when the connection is completed and also the committing of its disposition, because that Planet with which the disposition is perfected is the ruler of the thing and its doer.

Similarly about things in general, when the disposition comes to the Planet that receives it, the thing is improved and perfected by the will of God. And also, when it comes to a benefic, it perfects it by the same disposition. And when its disposition is completed and it has committed it to another [Planet], that dispositor will work through the quantity of its nature, and what there is of it, by the will of God. And Mercury was being joined to Venus after his exit from Aries, and Venus was receiving him from Taurus, and also he was being joined to Jupiter, and Jupiter was receiving her, and he was being received by her.

---

[1]That is, its readiness to occur or its slowness to occur.

Another Question about Life.

Another Question, of which Leo was the ASC in the 28th degree; and the MC was in Taurus the 20th degree; and Saturn was in Aries 4 degrees and 45 minutes; and the Moon in Aries 28 degrees and 27 minutes; and Jupiter in Taurus 9 degrees and 13 minutes; and Mars in Taurus 15 degrees and 18 minutes; and the Sun in Aquarius 24 degrees and 35 minutes; and Mercury in Aquarius 2 degrees[1] and 16 minutes direct; and Venus in Capricorn 11 degrees and 39 minutes.[2] So it is shown in this figure.

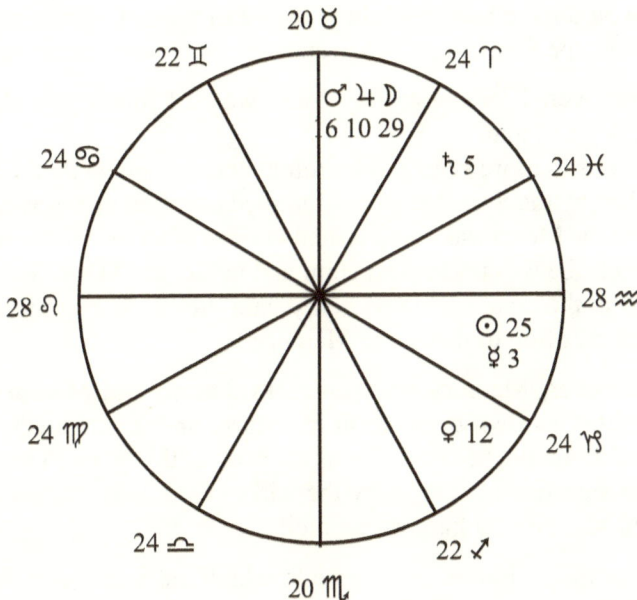

---

[1]So the text, but the chart has 4 degrees.

[2]The figure was presumably set for Baghdad at about 5:45 PM LAT (=6:01 PM LMT) on Sunday 13 February 791. The planetary positions were calculated from tables based on a fixed zodiac. *Surya Siddhanta* positions would agree closely for the Sun, Moon, and Mercury, and would be within one or two degrees for the others. The cuspal degrees are those shown in the chart in the printed book and are of course (except for the MC and the ASC) not original.

I looked at this Question, by the will of God; and the ASC was Leo; and the Sun was in the 7th sign, namely in the House of Marriage, *void of course*, i.e. joined to no [Planet]. I also looked at the Moon, which I found *void of course*, namely joined to no [Planet]. Therefore, I looked to see which of them was stronger in its place; and both of them were aspecting the ASC. But the Sun was in an angle, stronger than the rest.

I also looked to see which of them had more degrees in the sign in which it was, and which of them would more swiftly go out of its own sign; and it was the Moon. And I would have worked by her first; or if both of them would have been conjoined; or if the Sun would have been conjoined to one of them, I would have begun from the Sun, which was in an angle, but it was *void of course*.

Moreover, I looked at the Moon, which I found to be having more degrees than the Sun, and it was going to go out of the sign that it was in more swiftly. I therefore chose to judge by the Moon and then by the Sun. After that, I looked at which one of the seven Planets the Moon was being joined to first on her exit from the sign in which she was to the next sign; and in fact the Moon was being joined in the next sign to Mercury; and the Moon committed her own disposition to that same Mercury.

Moreover, Mercury was joined to Saturn; and Mercury also committed its own disposition to Saturn, and it was received by him by domicile, because he was the ruler of that place. Therefore, Saturn signified his health by the will of God, because Saturn received Mercury by his own domicile.

After that, I looked at the one to which the Sun would first be joined when it went out into the next sign; and the Sun would be joined to Jupiter, which is the ruler of the House of Death, but it was receiving the Sun by its own domicile. The Sun also signified health and good fortune, by the will of God, on account of the reception of the one that was receiving him. And if Jupiter would not have received him, that would have been a testimony of death, because Jupiter would have been the ruler of the House of Death.

And when the ruler of the House of Life is joined to the ruler of the House of Death, and when it commits its own disposition to him, it will signify death, by the will of God, unless there is some other thing that God wishes. For whether a benefic is the ruler of the House of Death or a malefic, it signifies death, because it is contrary to the ruler of the house of Life, unless there is reception that gives death between those, such as if the ruler of the House of Death, namely, receives the ruler of the House of Life, or it receives the disposer of the disposition for itself from the ruler of the House of Life, because then it is a strong reception.

And if the ruler of the House of Life receives the ruler of the House of Death, that will be a weak reception, but nevertheless the ruler of the House of Death does not destroy him totally, by the will of God. After that, look to see if you find the ruler of the House of Life and the Moon, both of them, signifying health; and if the stronger one of them is in its own place, then the other one will participate with it. But if you find one of them signifying life and the other one death, the signification of the ruler of life will be stronger and more dignified, because it does not suffer a detriment to life unless by the detriment of both; and the ruler of the House of Life is of more significance to that thing than the Moon.

But they are always partners in every thing; and properly, neither of them does anything without its partner; and therefore, when one of them perfects [the thing] and the other one experiences detriment, that will necessarily enter upon the one that perfects, and upon the thing [itself] according to the amount of the detriment of its partner.

And know that when you look into death and sickness, that before all the Planets the ruler of the House of Death and the ruler of the House of Sickness are more inimical to the House of Life, unless it is one and the same ruler, namely the ruler of Life and the ruler of Death; then it will not impedite itself, even if it is also a malefic, but the rest of the malefic Planets will impedite it.

And know that whichever one of the seven Planets that you find to be the ruler of the House of Life will not impedite itself; [even] if, that is, that one of them is a malefic. But the rest of the malefics may impedite it.

And know that which ever Planet you find to be the ruler of the House of Death is an enemy of the ruler of the House of Life, even if it is a benefic; nevertheless, it destroys the life if it is the dispositor, unless it receives or is received, then it takes away that [danger], by the will of God.

Also, the ruler of Life does not impedite itself whether it is a benefic or a malefic, even if Saturn or Mars would be the ruler of the House of Life. And the ruler of the House of Death is not friendly with another ruler of life, unless by reception, because death is inimical to life, unless there is a single ruler of them. Then it should be seen to which the ruler commits its own disposition, namely, the House of Death and the House of Life, or which is joined to it, committing to itself its own disposition.

And judge according to this: if it, namely the ruler of the House of Death and the ruler of the House of Life, commits its own disposition to a malefic Planet that is not receiving it, it will signify his death, if God wills it. And if it commits its own disposition to a malefic Planet, and that malefic receives it, he will be freed by the will of God. And if the ruler of Life and the ruler of the House of Death commit their own disposition to a benefic, the sick person will be freed from death, by the will of God; and a benefic will not impedite it, whether it receives it or it does not receive it.

After that, I looked for the lessening of the sickness and for its worsening; I looked namely at the ruler of the House of Sickness from the House of Sickness of this sick person, and it was Saturn which is not joined to and is not separated from any of them, because it is weightier than all [the rest].

I therefore looked at which of the seven Planets would be joined to it, or which of them would be separated from Saturn; namely, which one was more dignified in sickness; and I found Venus separated from Saturn, which was the ruler of the house of Sickness, by 7 degrees, and she was being joined to Mars who receives her, and she receives him—he receives her, namely by his own exaltation, and she receives him by her own domicile; both of them, therefore, signified a lessening of pain and the arrival of health, by the will of God. Look in this way at pain and death.

Questions of the Second House, and first about Finding or not Finding Wealth and what it will Amount to.

But if you want to know about wealth—what it will amount to—and if someone has asked you whether he might find wealth or not; and the Question is unqualified,[i.e.] of which the house is not known, and which is not being sought by another person, look at it from the ASC and the Moon, and from the House of Wealth, which is the second from the ASC.

Therefore, when you have established the ASC and its degree, look at the ruler of the House of Life, and if you find it aspecting the ascending sign, or if any one of the Planets is returning its own light to the ASC, work with it. But if that is not so, and the Moon is just as I have already said to you about the ruler of the ASC, work with her.

And if neither of them should aspect the ASC and they should not be joined to a Planet that returns their light to the ASC, you will take note of the one that has more degrees in the sign in which it is, and which one should more swiftly go out to the 2nd sign; then work through that one. But if the stronger one of them is joined to the ruler of the House of Wealth, which is the ruler of the 2nd house, he will find wealth and he will get it; whether it is received by the ruler of the house of Wealth or it is not received, [and] whether it is a benefic or a malefic, because the connection of the ruler of the ASC or the Moon with the ruler of the thing is the attainment of the thing by itself, and nothing forbids its effect, if God is willing, unless the ruler of the House of Wealth commits its own disposition to another Planet.

Then, it should be seen whether it is a malefic and receives the

House of Wealth, [if so] the thing will be perfected; and if it is a benefic, it will also be perfected, and he will find wealth, whether it is received or not received, if the dispositor itself is in a strong [place] or in the angles; for reception accomplishes the thing, and in no way can it be done without that being done; or without that same thing being prolonged or shortened, i.e either the time [for it] is long or it is short; but angles hasten the thing and strengthen it and are useful to the 2nd house.

Moreover, the cadent houses that do not aspect the ASC[1] delay the thing and postpone it, and they make delay; but reception cannot be annulled even if it delays, by the will of God. But if the ruler of the ASC or the Moon, namely either one of those, is joined to the ruler of the house of Wealth, or if a benefic is in the House of Wealth, or a malefic Planet that has a part, i.e. a dignity in the House of Wealth, which ever one does not receive the ruler of the ASC, or if there is a malefic Planet in the House of Wealth that does not have a part, i.e. a dignity, in that same house, and it would receive the ruler of the ASC; the thing [quesited] will be.

And if the ruler of the 2nd house, which is the House of Wealth, or a Planet that is in that same house is joined to the ruler of the ASC, the thing is done without any difficulty, and it will be perfected, by the will of God. The connection of the ruler of the ASC with Planets signifies the seeking of the thing from the ruler of the Question before it is given.

And the connection of the ruler of the House of Wealth with the ruler of the House of Life signifies that the thing will come without any seeking, and there will be more from that direction than is hoped for.

But if the ruler of the ASC and the Moon are not joined to the ruler of the 2nd house, nor to any Planet that is in its place—that is, which is descending into that same house. Then look at the one to which the ruler of the ASC or the Moon is joined; which, if they were both, or one of them, joined to a benefic, and if that Planet

---

[1]Namely, the 6th and the 12th houses.

would not commit its disposition to another [Planet], and it is in an angle or in a strong place, the thing will be perfected, and [the Querent] will find wealth, [whether] that benefic would receive it or would not receive it.

And if the ruler of the ASC or the Moon is joined to a malefic, if it receives it, the thing will be perfected; and if it does not receive it, it will be destroyed if the malefic itself is its dispositor and author, because a malefic Planet makes a detriment of things if it does not receive, and the benefics render those more useful, by the will of God, even if they do not receive; for if they do receive, the good will be greater; and if they do not receive, they [still] work good, and they do not impedite, by the will of God.

But if a benefic commits its own disposition to a malefic that does not receive it, the thing will experience the detriment of it when the disposition comes to the malefic; but if it receives it, the thing will be perfected.

A Question about Money borrowed—to be repaid, or to be given to You from his own [wealth].

Moreover, if you seek from someone wealth which you have borrowed or sought, so that he might give it to you from his own wealth, or in whatever way you have demanded it, the ruler of the ASC and the Moon will be the Querent, and the one from whom it is sought will be the ruler of the seventh; and the House of Wealth of the Querent will be the 2nd house from the ASC. Also, the House of Wealth of the one from whom it is asked will be the 2nd from the 7th, i.e. the 8th from the ASC, which is the House of Death.

But if the ruler of the ASC or the Moon is joined to the ruler of the House of Death, which is the ruler of the House of Wealth of the one from whom it is sought, or if it is joined to a Planet that is in that same house, just as I have said to you in the preceding chapter, he will acquire his own thing that he seeks.

And if there is no case of connection between it and the ruler of the House of Wealth of the aforesaid debtor, i.e. between the ruler of the ASC and the ruler of the House of Death, and it is not joined to any Planet that is in that same house, just as I have said before in the previous chapter. And the ruler of the House of Death, which is the ruler of the House of Wealth of the quesited, is not joined to the ruler of the ASC or to any Planet that is in the ASC, agreeing with itself, whether it is a malefic or a benefic, and its agreement is a reception, and so that there is any dignity for it in the ASC; then look at the one to which the ruler of the ASC or the Moon is joined, because if any one of them or if both of them are joined to a malefic planet that receives them or to a benefic that is in a strong place, the thing will be perfected, and he will find it, by the will of God.

A Question whether he will have the Wealth of a King or not.

And if the Questioner has asked you about wealth that is in the House of Wealth of a King,[1] whether he may have it or not, look for it according to what you have seen at his House of Wealth, i.e. of the aforesaid Querent; and at the House of Wealth of the aforesaid thing quesited, i.e. from the 11th [house]; and judge according to that, by the will of God.

A Question about the Time of having the Thing; namely, when that Thing will be had.

But if he has asked you when that will be, look at the planet to which the ruler of the ASC or the Moon is joined, or at the planet that is joined to the ruler of the ASC, or to a benefic that is closest to reception by the ruler of the ASC or the Moon, or at a malefic that receives the ruler of the ASC or the Moon in the very house of the thing signified—namely, the one that signified the effecting of the thing.

Then, if the effecting of the thing is by a connection of the known aspects, and not by body, look at when the ruler of the ASC or the Moon will project its own light partilely on the significator; and make the time to be according to the number of degrees that is between them, i.e. however many degrees there may be, put that many days.

---

[1]That is, the 2nd house from the 10th house.

But if it is not then, it will be when the ruler of the ASC or the Moon comes to the significator itself and is joined partilely to it by its own body in the sign in which it is; or when the significator comes to the ruler of the ASC, if there is a conjunction between them in one sign, and the ruler of the ASC is heavier, then the thing will be, by the will of God. And this will be in a strong place in the angles, or in a place in which the ruler of the thing rejoices.

But if it is not in that same hour, it will be when the author of the thing comes to the Sun, and it is oriental, i.e. when it has begun to rise after its own exit from being under the Sun beams; for then it will be renewed, and it will renew its own thing, if God wills it. And if it is under the Sun beams, it will be when it comes out from under the Sun beams; look at the day when this will be by the degrees which are between both of them, if they should be lighter stars—the Moon, namely, and Mercury and Venus and the Sun; put days for them according to that which is between them in degrees, until one of them projects its own light on another partilely, which is a true connection; then, there will be seen the degree in which the author of the thing is when it is joined to him seeking the thing partilely.

And when the degree of the ruler of the ASC or the Moon comes to it, the thing will be perfected, by the will of God. Of which thing, an example is, if some man would permit another man [to put] the thing in another place, and after that he would say this: "I shall put it here for you," and he would put it; afterwards he would set forth, and he would leave it in that same place until his lord would come, and would find it and accept it. But if it is not in the named place, he seeks until he comes to it, i.e. at the time promised; and when he comes to it, if he finds it in a place of his own strength, he will perfect his own thing, by the will of God.

Similarly, you should make the ruler of the ASC [to signify perfection] if the ruler of the thing is joined to it. And I shall put for you the likeness [of that] by which you will choose, and by which you will direct, if God wills it.

A Question about Inheritance

A Question about the things of a certain deceased person, about his Relicts, about which his neighbor asked, "Whether he would have anything from them or not?"

Of which the stars were in this manner. The ASC was Taurus 28 degrees, and the MC was Aquarius 13 degrees; and Venus in Aquarius 16 degrees and 41 minutes. And the Moon in Leo 28 degrees and 48 minutes; and Mercury in Pisces 19 degrees and 15 minutes; and the Sun in Aries 1 degree and 20 minutes; and Jupiter in Taurus 14 degrees and 15 minutes; and Mars in Gemini 6 degrees and 30 minutes.[1] Just as is plain in this figure.

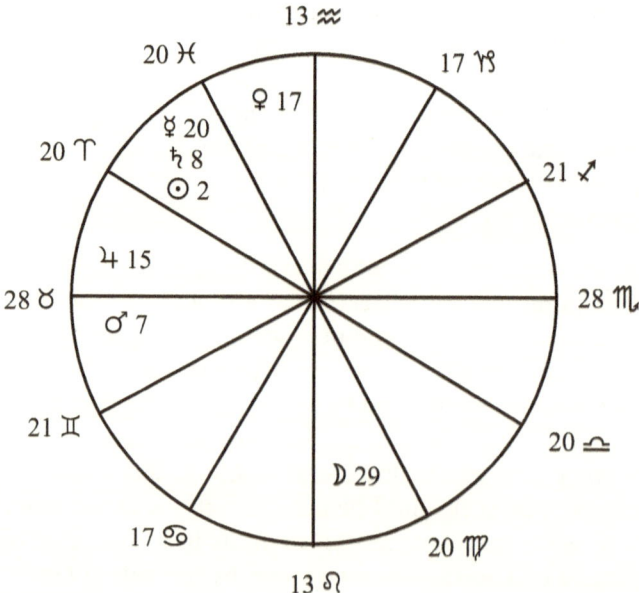

---

[1] The figure was presumably set for Baghdad at about 8:45 AM LAT (=8:51 AM LMT) on Tuesday 22 March 791. The planetary positions were calculated from tables based on a fixed zodiac. *Surya Siddhanta* positions would agree closely for Mars and Jupiter, and would be within a few degrees of the others. The position of

I looked at this Question, by the will of God; and the stars were just as I have said to you. Venus, namely was the ruler of the ASC, and she was *void of course*, conjoined to none; but she was separated from Jupiter, who was the ruler of the House of the Wealth of a dead person,[1] which is the 8th house from the ASC; and it was Jupiter in Taurus in her own domicile, and she was separated from him by reception; and separation by reception is something foul and a horrible thing.

After this I looked at the Moon in the same hour, which was also separated from Venus; I therefore looked at their places, and I found both of them in angles aspecting the ASC; and I looked at the one that had more degrees in its own sign, which ought to more swiftly go out of it. And they were both in angles, but the Moon was the one that ought to go out more swiftly; and she had more degrees in her own sign, which I changed to the second sign in her own place, and she is joined first to Mars; and Mars is a malefic and does not receive her; and Mars is not received by her. And Mars was not the ruler of the House of Wealth of the Dead, which is the house of the thing of the Querent; it therefore signified the prohibition of the thing.

After that, I also changed Venus to the following sign; Venus also signified that which the Moon had signified, because it was joined first to Mars, But if Mars would have been the ruler of the House of Wealth of the Dead and had received Venus or the Moon, and if it would have been a benefic, and if it would have been in an angle or in a place of its own strength, I would have said that the thing would be perfected, and that he would acquire some of the wealth of that same deceased person.

And if in the House of Wealth of the Dead, there would have been a benefic, or a malefic would have been joined to it; and if it

---

Saturn is not given, but Mâshâ°allâh would probably have put it in about Aries 7 degrees and 45 minutes. The cuspal degrees are those shown in the chart in the printed book and are of course (except for the ASC and the MC) not original.

[1] Here he assumes that the dead person is ruled by the 7th house because it is the House of the person asked about. Hence, that person's wealth is represented by the 8th House.

would have had any dignity in that same house, and if it would have received Venus, or if it would not receive if Venus would be joined to it; or if there would be a malefic Planet in the same house receiving Venus or the Moon having no dignity in that same place, the thing would be if Venus were joined to it, because reception will not perish in whatever manner it exists, by the will of God.

And when the Planet that rules the thing receives and is its dispositor, and comes to its disposition and commits it to another, the thing will be; but if it commits it to another after its own reception, the reception will signify the perfection of the thing; and the committing of its own disposition to another signifies the end of the thing, and to what the last of it will come; because perfection, i.e. the performance of a thing is perhaps known from the Planet to which the ruler of the ASC is first joined; from the Moon; or from the second one that receives the commitment [of the disposition], or namely from whichever one is the last reception [and] there will be the end; or from the ruler of the thing quesited; or from a benefic that is in a good place without reception. And so the Planets signify that which they signify in their own places; and it was from despair of it that the ruler of his Question sought it.

And the hour in which he already understood that it would not be done [was] when Venus went out of Aquarius into the second sign from her own place, which is the sign Pisces; and when the Moon was joined to Venus by her own body; after that she was separated from Venus and joined to Mars partilely from Pisces. In that same hour, he despaired of that which he had sought, because the Moon is the significator of things; and she was joined to Mars; but before Venus changed in the hour of the Question, because the Moon was with Mars, [but] before that Venus was joined to it.

And when the rumor had come to Venus, the Moon indicated the rumor to be one of Venus; after that the Moon was joined to Mars by body; and from that there came the detriment of the thing, and the thing was destroyed then and dissolved. And know that angles strengthen a thing and hurry and fortify a thing, whether good or evil; therefore, whatever of good there is attached to its own ruler and will last; and whatever of evil there is will last similarly for the one suffering it.

A Question of the Tenth House. And first about a Kingdom, for one Asking if he will have it or not, and when.

But if you have been asked about a kingdom, and a man has asked you whether he will rule or not, and his Question is unqualified, i.e. he does not say to you whether he will rule in this year or in this month or in this week, look at him, if you see that he will rule, and he says to you, "when does it seem to you that this can be done?" You should fix for him the time according as you see it in your [chart for the] Question, i.e. you will predict for him when that will be in his own life, namely in some part of that same life.

And in general, Questions of this sort will be [the same] in all things; but if he asks you about the year or the month, or less than that or more, and you see that it will not be done, make your reply that it is not [going to] be known in that same time about which he asked; and if he [then] asks you when it will be known about that thing, tell him when it will be from the [chart of the] hour in which he asked you.

And if you see that the thing will be done, indicate to him when it will be from the time about which he asked in the beginning, namely either in the middle or at the end of it, or it will be in some hour of that. The knowledge of which thing you will acquire thus: establish namely the ASC and the MC and their degrees by the ascensions of your own city in which you then were, and by equal hours, and with the general [rules] that are necessary for the thing which is asked about. Therefore, set for it the ASC by equal hours. After that, look at the ruler of the ASC and the Moon, which are always for the Querent for all men and all Questions, whether a man or a woman is the Querent, and whether [the Querent] is lowly or great.

After that, look at which one is stronger, the ruler of the ASC or the Moon; and see whether the stronger one of them is joined to the ruler of the MC, or whether it receives the ruler of the MC, which is the House of the King, and if the ruler of the House of the King is not committing its own disposition[1] to another [Planet], then the Querent will get his own thing—namely, he will find the kingdom that he asked about; or if the ruler of the MC receives the ruler of the ASC, whether it is a benefic or a malefic, then the Querent seeking the thing and the kingdom gets his own thing, by the will of God.

But if the ruler of the MC was receiving the ruler of the ASC or the Moon, then it is good, because it will be better and stronger and it will more [readily] move the thing to what may be done, and it will be more stable and durable. But if the ruler of the MC is the one that is joined, i.e. if it is seeking a connection with the ruler of the ASC, then he will acquire the asked about kingdom without any seeking for it; on the other hand, it will not come to him sitting in his own house and without effort. For if the ruler of the ASC is joined to the ruler of the MC, it can be done when he [actively] seeks it, or when someone [does] it for him, because the connection with the ruler of the ASC is itself [indicative of] acquisition; and reception is choosing.

And if the connection is by opposition or by square aspect, there will be some difficulty and delay or labor in [acquiring] the thing. But if the connection is by trine or sextile aspect, the thing will be without labor and without difficulty. It is done similarly in the case of a connection by body.

But if the ruler of the ASC or the Moon is not joined to the ruler of the MC, and the ruler of the MC is not joined to it; and if there is not any one of the Planets between them committing its disposition until it brings it to them, then look at the ruler of the ASC or the Moon; if the stronger one of them is joined to another that is not the ruler of the kingdom, i.e. the ruler of the MC, and that Planet is a benefic, or it is in an angle, or in a strong place, the thing will be perfected, by the will of God, whether it receives it or does not receive it.

---

[1] Reading *dispositionem* 'disposition' instead of *desperationem* 'desperation'.

And if it is a malefic, and it receives it, the thing will be perfected, if God wills it. But if it is a malefic and it is not the ruler of the MC, and it does not receive the ruler of the ASC, and the malefic itself does not commit its own disposition to another malefic that receives the ruler of the ASC, and that malefic will not give its own disposition to another malefic that receives the ruler of the ASC, and that malefic does not give its own disposition to another Planet, then the thing will not be perfected, because that malefic destroys it, by the will of God; and if that malefic commits its own disposition to a benefic that is in a strong place, the thing will be perfected, by the will of God.

After this, look at that Planet which is in the sign of the MC or in the sign of the ASC.[1] If there is a malefic Planet in the sign of the MC, and it does not have any dignity in it, and it receives the ruler of the ASC or the Moon, the thing will be perfected; and if it does not receive it, it will not be perfected.

And if the exaltation of that same malefic is in the sign of the MC, and it is [thus] in its own exaltation, the thing will be perfected by the will of God [if] it receives the ruler of the ASC and the Moon, [or] whether or not it receives it, if God wills it. And if there is a benefic in the sign of the MC, and there is joined to it the Moon or the ruler of the ASC, the thing will be perfected by the will of God, whether that benefic receives it or not, [or] whether that benefic has dignity in the sign of the MC or not.

Look also at the connection of the ruler of the MC with Planets that are in the ASC, just as you have looked in the case of the ruler of the ASC and its connection with the stars that are in the sign of the MC. And know that Planets that rule the thing in the 4 angles arrange the thing, and hurry it up, and excite it; and they perfect the things quesited.

---

[1]This would seem to indicate the use of the Sign-House system of house division.

A Question about the Good or Evil that exists in a thing or is expected to exist in it afterwards.

But if he has asked you about good or evil, that exists in a thing or is expected to exist in it afterwards; and you find the Planets that rule the thing in the angles, that good or evil will be durable. And look at the connection of the Planets that are in the angles and their reception, and they are helpers for this in connection with your own thing, if God wills.

A Question about when Someone will have a Kingdom, or when he will be Deprived of it.

And if some uneasy person has asked when that kingdom will be, look at the ruler of the ASC and the Moon, which of them is stronger in signifying the attainment of the thing; and work through it. Look, namely, at the stronger one of them, i.e. the one that is stronger between the ruler of the ASC and the Moon; and see how many degrees are between the stronger of them and the planet that perfects its thing until it is joined to it partilely; and put those [degrees] as days.

But if it is not [perfected] then, it will be when the ruler of the ASC or the Moon comes to it and is joined to it by its own body in one degree; or when the ruler of the ASC or the Moon comes to the degree in which the ruler of the MC was, and [if] it was strong in the place, i.e. received in the angles, or in the best place in the middle houses, i.e. in those following the angles[1]; and if there is some dignity to it in that same place; then it will be.

Then, know that the strength of a place, i.e. strong places in which the one perfecting the thing and preparing it rejoices, will indicate to you when the thing about which you were asked will be, by the will of God. That is, you should see to which one the ruler of the ASC or the Moon is joined partilely. And you should know in what degree the author of the thing is.

But if when it projects its own rays partilely upon it, and [the

[1]That is, in the *succedent* houses.

thing] does not occur, it will [then] be when it comes to the degree in which the aforesaid author was, if the author is in a strong place and has in it any sort of strength in which it rejoices. But if then too it is not [perfected] when the ruler of the ASC comes to it or aspects it, and the author itself is in a strong place, it will be then, by the will of God. But if that about which you were asked is not [perfected], and you see that it is not done, look then at the Planet that signified an impediment to the thing and the loss of hope for it.

And so, look at this, just as you have looked at that which perfected it, and when it would be. If you see what is being done, then there will be a loss of hope for that same thing, by the will of God. And if the ruler of the ASC or the Moon is joined to the author by their own body in one sign, and the author is in the angles, look at how many degrees there are between them, and put them as days if they are light stars; and if they are heavy stars, put down months in accordance with the number of degrees; and it will be according to that same number, if God wills it.

And know that the light stars are the Moon, Mercury, Venus, and the Sun; but the heavy ones are Saturn, Jupiter, and Mars. And now I am putting an example for you that you ought to know.

A Question about getting a Kingdom

A certain man asked whether or not he would get a kingdom that he had sought for himself. [The Question] had also been put forth and stated by himself; and the ASC sign of it was Gemini, the 5th degree, and the MC was Aquarius the 10th degree. And Mercury was in Gemini the 14th degree and the 46th minute retrograde; and the Moon in Sagittarius the 9th degree and 18th minute; and the Sun in Gemini the 51st minute; and Jupiter in Taurus the 28th degree and the 43rd minute. And Saturn in Aries the 16th degree; and Venus in Aries the 24th degree and 42nd minute; and Mars in Cancer the 11th degree and 58th minute; just as is shown in this figure.[29]

---

[29]The figure was presumably set for Baghdad at about 5:15 AM LAT (=5:09 AM LMT) on Monday 23 May 791. The planetary positions were calculated from tables based on a fixed zodiac. *Surya Siddhanta* positions would agree closely

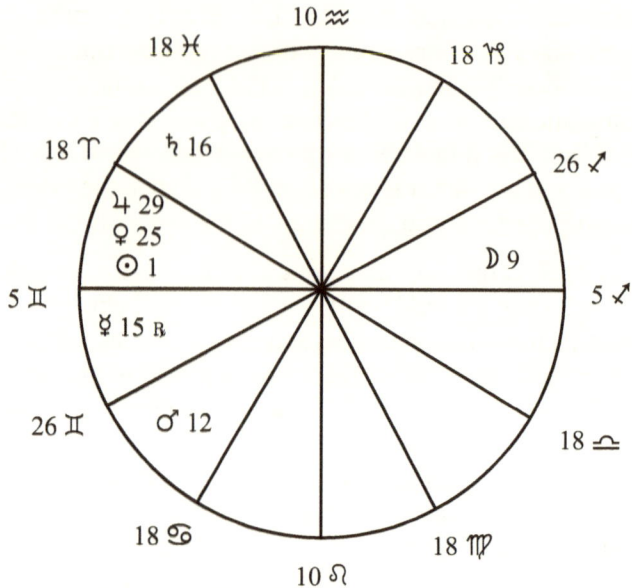

I looked at this Question, by the will of God. And Mercury was the ruler of the ASC and retrograde, for it would return to the Sun and be joined to it; and the Sun was seeking a connection with Saturn by sextile aspect; and Mars was going to Saturn to be joined to it by a square aspect; and all of them were in aspect, and therefore they were having testimonies, but Mars conquered, i.e. he came to Saturn first and was joined to him partilely, which is a true connection; and he cut off the connection of the Sun from Saturn, and he destroyed the thing; and Mars destroyed it, because he separated the Sun and Saturn.

And the Sun was the one to whom the ruler of the ASC and the Moon were committing their disposition; and he was in the middle

for the Sun, Mercury, Jupiter, and Saturn, and would be within a few degrees for the others. The cuspal degrees are those shown in the chart in the printed book and are of course (except for the ASC and MC) not original.

between the ruler of the MC, which is the ruler of the thing that he was seeking, and the ruler of the ASC; and if Mars would not have cut off the connection between the Sun and Saturn, and if the Sun would have been joined to Saturn before Mars would have been joined to it, the thing would have been perfected by the will of God. But Mars was in a place in which it was joining to Saturn, and the Sun was joined to it; and Mars destroyed the thing when it separated between the Sun and Saturn and cut off their connection. Mars was therefore joined to Saturn, and the Sun was joined to none; and the light of Mars separated between it and Saturn, which is the ruler of the thing of the Question.

I also wanted to know when that loss of hope would be; i.e. when it would be plain to him that what he had asked about would not be done; and that was when Mars was joined to Saturn and cast its own light partilely on Saturn itself. And on that same day there was the loss of hope about that thing.

And know that when the Moon is in the sign of the MC joined to the ruler of the ASC, the thing will also be perfected, by the will of God, because it is in the place of the thing. And if it is the significator of things, and it is fortunate, the thing will also be perfected, by the will of God, whether it is received or not, even if the ruler of the ASC were Saturn or Mars. And know that the accomplishment of things is perhaps in the beginning of the connection, or in its middle, or in the end—namely, whichever one is in agreement and in reception.

And the perfection of a thing is from the *Almuten* or from the author, to which comes the last one of the dispositions and connections; and it is the *Almuten*; or the author itself, always receiving the one who commits his disposition to it, and is concordant with the thing; then the thing will be perfected, and it will not experience detriment, whether it was prolonged or happens swiftly, by the will of God.

Another Question about a Kingdom.

A certain man asked whether or not he would acquire a kingdom in that same year. And the ASC was Cancer the 24th degree; and the MC was Aries the 3rd degree; and the Moon was in Libra in the 4th degree and the 22nd minute; and Saturn in Aries in the 11th degree; and the Sun in Aries in the 29th degree and the 11th minute; and Venus in Pisces in the 17th degree and the 9th minute' and Jupiter in Taurus in the 21st degree and the 40th minute; and Mercury in Taurus in the 10th degree and the 15th minute; and Mars in Gemini in the 22nd degree and the 26th minute. Just as is shown in this figure.[1]

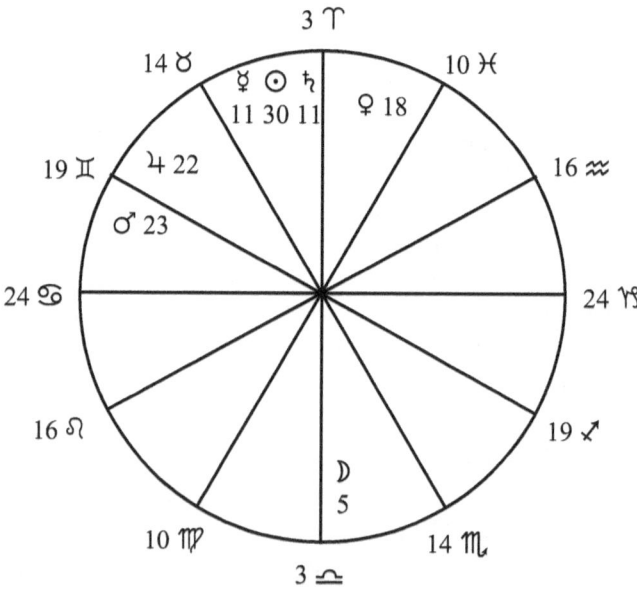

---

[1]The figure was presumably set for Baghdad on Thursday 21 April 791 at about 11:00 AM LAT (= 10:57 LMT). The MC should be 13 ♈ instead of 3 ♈ (or else the ASC should be 17 ♑)The house cusps are those shown in the chart in the printed book and (other than the MC and the ASC) are of course not original. The Planetary positions are based on a fixed zodiac as mentioned before.

Therefore, in this Question I looked, by the will of God, at the ruler of the ASC; and it was the Moon, which I found connected to Saturn in Libra, namely in his own exaltation. And Saturn received the Moon from his own exaltation; and it signified the completion of the thing by the will of God, because Saturn received the Moon, which was the ruler of the ASC, and Saturn was in the House Royal, which is the place of the thing; and its rulership was from the reception by Saturn, because it was receiving the Moon; but this will not be unless it is sought from the ruler of the Question; and there will be some hardship or labor there, because Saturn receives the Moon from an opposition and contrariety; and the mind of the one seeking the thing will be troubled on account of his own place, because Saturn that received the Moon is in his own fall and in a pit[1] and in his own debility; and Saturn is troubled in his own place, because we have seen that that man will be troubled in his own effort; and he will be hated on account of the [natural] hatred of Saturn, which it has against its own place, because Saturn is the one that bestows the kingdom on him by the will of God; and his own condition and his nature is just like the nature of Saturn and the essence of Saturn. And the ruler of the Question will find with him the one that establishes the place of the reception and the honor and the selection, because Saturn is the ruler of the 7th from the ASC, and he receives the ruler of the ASC; and the ruler of the ASC is the Querent; but the ruler of the 7th is the one who arranged [the Question] for the Querent; therefore, because it is connected to him and received by him, we have said that there will be good relations between them; and a reception with a good place will be with him, if God wills it.

And when you want to know when this man's kingdom will be, look at how many degrees are between the Moon and Saturn until she is joined to it partilely by her own light; and there was 6 degrees between them; there would therefore be 6 days; but if it was not then, it will be when the Moon comes to the same degree in

---

[1]The pits of the sign Aries are the 6th, 11th, 16th, 23rd, and 29th degrees. See the table in William Lilly, *Christian Astrology* (London: Partridge & Blunden, 1647; repr. Exeter: Regulus, 1985.), p. 116.

which Saturn was, when he receives the Moon partilely by his own light. And if it was not then, it will be when Venus comes to the degree of the ASC, because Venus is the ruler of the domicile of the Moon, because it is the sign of Libra in which the Moon was, and the Moon was the ruler of the ASC.

And know that the ruler of the ASC and the Moon, when they are both cadent, would at least perfect their own work and their own disposition. And if the thing which you have foreseen does not occur; you must work through the ruler of the sign in which the ruler of the ASC is. Therefore, the rulership of that man was at 90 days from the day on which the Question was put; that is, when Venus first came into a degree of the ASC of the ascending sign[1]; for she came into a place that was strong and conformable to the thing, and it was done then, by the will of God.

And the stars operate then by the will of God, for good or evil, when they are in a strong place in the higher houses and the fixed signs, because those are the ones that fix and confirm things, both good and evil, by the will of God; and they also set them in motion at the time of their own completion. Therefore, set your own heart to knowing the falling of the Planets from the angles,[2] and their elevation, or their sublimity in those angles for the movement [forward] of things and their moving back, or their stability, and their confirmation.

And if there was not any rulership for that man when Venus comes to the degree of the ASC in the east, I would say that it would be when Venus comes to the degree of the fourth sign, or to the degree of the seventh, or to the degree in which Saturn was at the hour of the Question, or when the Sun comes to Saturn and it would be made oriental, and it would go out from under the Sun beams, and it would be renewed, and it would renew the thing that it rules.

---

[1] Mâshâ>allâh must have meant that after 90 days Venus would come to a degree of the ASC sign. If so, he was approximately correct, since by then it would then have come to about 4 ♋ (in his fixed zodiac).

[2] That is, when they are cadent.

And the coming of Venus to the degree in which the Moon was is a strong thing. Moreover, that man went out to the work that he ruled when Venus came to the degree of the ascending sign. And know that it was for this reason that the slowness of this thing occurred—because the Moon was in the fourth angle and was being joined to Saturn—from which you knew the accomplishment of the thing; and Saturn was in an angle in the 10th house—namely, the house of the thing—and in the House of Kingdom.

And if the Moon would have been in the 7th angle, it would have been done as a swifter thing. And if it would have been with Saturn in the 10th sign, it would have been still swifter; and if it had been in the ascending sign, it would have been swifter than in the rest of the houses. And know that the strength of the ruler of the ASC and the strength of the Moon make these things to be accelerated; or their debility makes them to be delayed if they are weak. For if they were in angles, and the Planet to which they are connected is similarly in an angle, it will hurry up the thing, by the will of God.

And if one of them was cadent and the other was in a strong house—that is the Planet to which it is connected—it will similarly impedite that thing; and it will make it to be delayed according to the quantity of its fall, and according to the impediment that enters upon it in the house in which it is. And know that Planets that are cadent from the angles cause everything to be delayed that has not yet occurred and is expected to be done. And Planets cadent from the angles are good and the best for every good thing for which a returning is expected, such as a journey, when a journey is looked at for a traveler, i.e. a wayfarer; or for a prefect or a King.

But when it is looked at [to see] when he will fall and lose his kingdom, or for an important man when he will lose his place in his own order, and for every good or evil person, when he will lose the rulership of his own place and be taken away from it, look at this from the recession of the strong Planets, which are strengthened in the four angles, of which the more dignified and swifter is the ASC in doing good things; and the second in accomplishment is the MC angle, namely the 10th; and the third is the 7th House of the Spouse and Marriage; and the fourth is the Angle of Earth, i.e. the House of Fathers.

But of the intermediate houses, the most dignified is the House of Hope; and it is swifter than the House of Marriage and the House of Fathers for doing things; and it is the 11th house; and second is the House of Travel, and it is the 9th; and the third is the House of Children, and it is the 5th; and the fourth is the House of Brothers, [which is] the 3rd; [and these] are good and praiseworthy.

The cadent houses are therefore worse than all the [other] houses—namely, the House of Death, which is the 8th; and the House of Sickness, which is the 6th; and the House of Enemies, which is the 12th; and the House of Wealth, which is the 2nd from the ASC. [And these] houses are inimical to the ASC, which they do not aspect; and they are the conclusion of this thing and [indicators] of little advancement; for I have not found in one of them anything but a small thing.

Nevertheless, he received the command, by the will of God; and its delay was until it returned to its own domicile in 15 days; and therefore the stability of his law occurred and the strength of his own work, because of the location of the Planets in the angles. And the smallness of his advance came therefore because Saturn, which gave him the kingdom, by the will of God, was in the sign of its own fall, and of its own evil and worthlessness and in a pit, in a place in which there was not dignity for it; and it was that which gave to itself something hateful on account of the hate that it was having for its own place; but it fixed all of its own things that were going to be fixed in the angles.

A Chapter on the Knowledge of the Life of the Native.

When you want to know the life of a native, by the will of God, if the birth was by day, begin with the Sun. If the Sun is in the ASC or in the MC, or in the adverse position, that is in the opposite position, which is the 7th from the ASC, or [else] in the 11th, and it does not go back from the degree of the house in which it is by more than 5 degrees; and it is received by the ruler of the domicile or of the sign of the exaltation in which it is from the connection, then it will be useful for the Hyleg.[1]

And the planet that receives will be the *alcochoden*;[2] and that one is the significator that rules the nativity, namely as the giver of years or months or days; and the division of months or years or days will be directed from the degree in which it is, and that is the degree of the Hyleg.

But if the Sun is not in any one of the houses that I have mentioned to you; or if it is in [one of] those, and it is removed from the degree of the house in which it is by more than 10 degrees; or it is in them, and there is not between it and the ruler of the domicile or the exaltation in which is the connection—[i.e.] if it is thus, it will not be useful as the Hyleg.

Therefore, ignore it and look at the Moon, which if it is in the 4 angles and in the succedents, which are the 2nd house and the 5th and the 8th [and the 11th]; these are 8 houses; and if it is not removed from the degree of the house that it is in by more than 5 degrees[3]; and it is conjoined to the ruler of the domicile or the exaltation in which it is, it will be useful as the Hyleg.

Direct then the division of years or months or days, by the will of God. But if the Moon is not then in one of those 8 houses that I

---

[1]From the Arabic *haylaj* from a Persian word. It corresponds to the *aphetic place* in a natal horoscope, which can be directed to determine the length of life. Thus it is similar to the *alcochoden* (see the next note). However, Leopold of Austria says that it defines the quality of life, while the *alcochoden* defines the length. But that is somewhat different from the Ptolemaic characterization of the *aphetic place* or Hyleg.

[2]Variously spelled in Latin, it is from the Arabic *al-kadkhudâh*, which is from a Persian word used to translate the Greek *oikodespotês* 'house-ruler', often used to signify the 'ruler of the nativity'. Here it corresponds to the "giver of years."

[3]By this he means that a Planet that is more than 5 degrees from the cusp and in the preceding house cannot be considered to be in the house of the cusp. For example, if the cusp of the 9th house is 20 Libra and a Planet is in 16 Libra, then it is in the 9th house; but if it is in 14 Libra, it is more than 5 degrees distant from the cusp, so it is in the 8th house and not in the 9th house. (This is Ptolemy's rule.)

have named for you; or if it is removed from the degree of the house that it is in by more than 5 degrees; or if it is not removed in them; and it is not joined to the ruler of the domicile or exaltation; then if it is thus, it will not be useful to become the Hyleg.

Look then at the degree of the Part of Fortune; if it falls in any one of those 8 houses; and it is not remote from the degree of the house in which it is by more than 5 degrees; and if the ruler of the terms of the degree of the Part of Fortune, or the ruler of its house is joined to it, it will be useful for the Hyleg[1] and for the houses of its terms; or the ruler of the house that is joined to it; it will rule, i.e. it will be the giver of years or months or days from the degree of the Part of Fortune to it.

But if it is not the ruler of the terms of the Part of Fortune, or the ruler of the house that is joined to it—that is, to the Part of Fortune—then the Part of Fortune [itself] will rule, and it will be the Hyleg; and from its ruler is known the giving of years and months or days; and from the degree of the Part of Fortune you will direct the division of it—namely, of months or days or years—by the will of God.

But if the Part of Fortune is not in these 8 houses; or it is in them but it is remote from the degree of the house that it is in by more than 5 degrees, it will not be useful; ignore it then.

But if the degree of the conjunction of the Sun and the Moon before the birth of the native is in one of these 8 houses, and it is not remote from the house in which it is by more than 5 degrees; and the ruler of its terms, or the ruler of the house in which it is, is joined to it, it will rule the signification of the giving of years or months or days from the degree of the conjunction, because it was made Hyleg by the will of God.

Moreover, if the native is born in the conjunction, and the ruler of its terms, or the ruler of the house in which it is, is not joined to the degree of the conjunction; and that conjunction is in the afore-

---

[1] Reading *hyleg* 'Hyleg' instead of *hile*.

said 8 houses and not removed from the house in which it is by more than 5 degrees, the conjunction will be the Hyleg; and its ruler will rule and also that conjunction—both of them namely—and from them is known the giving or years or months or days.

But if the degree of the conjunction of the Sun and the Moon is not in one of the aforesaid 8 houses, or if it is in one of them and is remote from the degree of the house by more than 5 degrees, it will not be useful to be the Hyleg; therefore, ignore it. Similarly, look at the degree of the preceding [phase] that is called the Full Moon, which was before the nativity, if it was a nativity [that occurred] in the aforesaid phase. Which degree, if it is in one of the aforesaid 8 houses and not remote from the degree in which it is by more than 5 degrees, it will be useful for the Hyleg; and from it direct the division of years or months or days. But if the ruler of its terms or the ruler of the house that is joined to it, the one of those that is joined to it will rule the nativity, which one will also signify the giving of years or months or days.

And if the degree of the Full Moon is in the aforesaid houses, not removed from the degree of the house in which it is by more than 5 degrees; but the ruler of its terms or the ruler of that house is not joined to it; then nevertheless the degree of the Full Moon will be the Hyleg, and it will rule; and from its place is known the giving of years or months or days; and from that same degree is directed the division of years or months or days, by the will of God. And if the degree of the full Moon is in one of those 8 houses, but it is removed from the degree of the house that it is in by more than 5 degrees, it will not be useful as Hyleg. Ignore it then, and look at the degree of the ASC, because it will be the Hyleg.

And the ruler of its terms or the ruler of the house that is joined to it will rule the nativity; and that one will be the giver and significator of years or months or days. And the division of years or months or days is directed from the degree of the ASC. But if the ruler of its terms or the ruler of the house is not joined to it, i.e. if neither of these is joined to the degree of the ascending sign, then the degree of the ASC itself will be the Hyleg, and it will rule the nativity; and from it is directed the division of years or months or days; and from it is known the giving of years or months or days.

And you will work at night[1] just as you work by day, the same way at all times; but you will begin by day from the Sun, then from the Moon, then from the Part of Fortune, then from the New Moon or the Full Moon if it is a nativity; and after that from the degree of the rising sign.

And when you have rejected those places in the previously mentioned chapters; and your own [chosen] place is from the degree of the ASC; the life of the child will not be prolonged unless the degree of the ASC is free from the projection of the light of the malefics on it—namely, of Saturn or of Mars—and you will not ignore it when you find this to be the ruler of the nativity, as you will look at the extensions of the rays of the Planets to the Hyleg; because something of the ray of the Planets is strong unless the Sun or Venus or Jupiter or the Moon is in aspect with them, because an aspect from these breaks the virtue of the malefics, if the malefics do not have more degrees than the benefics; and with this you should also not ignore the casting of the malefics onto the Hyleg by their own rays, even when it is the one that rules the nativity; [for] the strong ruler of the nativity will not perish, by the will of God.

A Chapter on the Years of the *Alcochoden*.

And when you find the one that rules the nativity in the ASC or in the MC or in the 7th angle, that has gone out from under the Sun beams, i.e. it is not under the Sun beams, it is direct, and it is not in its own fall, it will give its own major years. And if it is in the 4th angle, which is [the angle] under the earth, and in its own terms or in its domicile or in its exaltation or in its triplicity, and if it is oriental, it will give its own major years; and if it is in the 11th from the ASC or in the 5th, and it is oriental, and it is in its own terms or in its domicile or in its exaltation or in its triplicity or in its own face, it will give its own major years.

---

[1]That is, in nocturnal nativities or Questions.

And if it is in the 11th from the ASC or in the 5th, and it is oriental, and it is not in its own terms or in its domicile or in its exaltation or in its triplicity or in its own face, it will give its own middle years. And if it is in the 2nd from the ASC or in the 8th, and it is in its own terms or exaltation, or in its domicile or triplicity, or in its own face, it will give its own middling years; and if it is not in its own terms, nor in its exaltation of domicile, or in its triplicity or its own face, and it is not in its own fall, nor in a pit, or in a place in which it is sad, it will similarly give its own middling years. And if it is in the 9th from the ASC, and it is oriental in its own terms, or in its domicile or exaltation, or in its triplicity or its own face, it will give its own middling years.

If it is a diurnal nativity, and the one that rules [it] is diurnal; or if it is a nocturnal nativity, and the one that rules [it] is nocturnal; and if it is in the 6th from the ASC or in the 12th, and it is not in its own fall, it will give its own minor years; and if it is in its own fall in the 12th or in the 6th retrograde, it will give months according to the number of its own minor years, i.e. in place of each year, it will give a month. And if it is under the Sun beams, retrograde, in its own fall, and it is in the 12th from the ASC or in the 6th, it will give days according to the number of its own minor years, i.e. in place of each year, it will give a day.

And if you find the one that is the ruler of the nativity, namely retrograde in an angle or under the Sun beams, it will give its middling years. And if it is retrograde or under the Sun beams in a succedent, it will give its own minor years. And if it is cadent from the angles and it is retrograde under the Sun beams, it will not be able to give its minor years, but it will give a month in place of a year.

And when the one that rules [the nativity] gives the years, and all the benefics aspect it by a square aspect, or by opposition, or by sextile aspect or by trine, or when they are with it in one sign, they will increase it according to the quantity of degrees that are in the time of the hours of that degree in which it is—by one degree to a year. If the one that increases it is not retrograde nor under the Sun beams, and when there are planets that signify an increase in the 6th from the ASC or in the 12th, they will make no increase.

And if any one of the malefic planets aspects the one that rules [the nativity] by any aspect from the 4th namely, or the 10th, or from the 7th, or by sextile, or if it was with it—whichever it is—it will diminish it according to the number of degrees that are in the time of the hours of that degree in which it is in the clime in which the nativity is at [the rate of] one year per degree of the degrees of the temporal hours.

And I have found in a certain book, but I have not proved it, that when you find *Cauda*[1] with the one that rules the nativity no farther than 8 degrees from it, it will diminish by a fourth part the years of the one that rules; and if it is *Caput*[2] [placed] thus, it will similarly diminish a fourth part of the years. And know that the extension of the rays of the Planets is by equal degrees, but give the years to the Hyleg by ascensional degrees; and do not ignore the giving of years by the ASC by ascensional degrees. And know that when you have taken the giving of years or months or days from the degree of the Hyleg or from the degree of the ASC, for each degree there is a year or a month or a day.

And whenever you find a malefic, let it be seen where the degree comes that you have taken from[3] the Hyleg or from the ASC; and know that the degree to which the giving which you have taken from the Hyleg or from the degree of the ASC, if any of these four benefics aspect it, he will escape and be freed from death, unless there are malefic degrees that aspect the place from which comes the division by more degrees, i.e. if the malefic degrees have more degrees than the benefics; for this signifies that the native will last until those degrees that you have directed from the Hyleg cross the degrees of a benefic; and when they have crossed over those and have come to the malefic degrees, it will then signify death.

---

[1]The Tail of the Dragon or the South Node.
[2]The Head of the Dragon or the North Node.
[3]Reading *ab* 'from' instead of *ad* 'to'.

And know that when it is a nativity, and the one that rules it is in a strong place, if a malefic projects its own rays on the degree of the significator[1] of life or upon the degree of the Sun or the degree of the Moon or the degree of the Hyleg, which ever one it is, the native will be subject to death until the one that rules the nativity completes the number of years that it signified according to the quality of the place in which it is—namely, of its major years or its middling or minor ones, or months or days or hours, if God wills it.

And I shall explain to you the casting of rays. Understand it! Some think that the casting of rays is the same as a Planet, namely, that is in the 10th receiving the rays from the one that receives it from the fourth [sign] from it; and the one that is in the fourth [sign] from it projects its own rays on the one that is in the 10th from it; and therefore they call the casting of rays to be like the four modes that I have mentioned, because the one that is before it in the fourth [sign] has projected rays onto the one that is put after it in the 10th [sign] before that one that is in the fourth [sign], because that one that goes before it casts its own hot rays on the part that is after it similarly; because one that is in Aries aspects one that is in Caner; and the one that is in Cancer projects its own rays onto the one that is in Aries.

And the greater part of the wise men agree that you should put those five degrees that are before the degree of the ASC to be degrees of the strength of the ASC; in which, when the Sun is there, they say that it is useful to be made the Hyleg when it is received; and the Moon similarly, and the rest [of the Planets] from which the Hyleg is found similarly.[2]

Moreover, the one that is ruling, which signifies the giving of years, when it is remote from the degree of the ASC, and is in 5 degrees before the angle, they have said it cannot give its major years, but it can give its middling years; and it seems to us [proper] to adopt [the rule of] that book, so that the one that rules may be

---

[1]Reading *significatoris* 'significator' instead of *signi* 'sign'.
[2]Again, this is the rule stated by Ptolemy.

known and the Hyleg; after that it may be known, what it would signify of years or months or days or hours.

Therefore, when we have recognized which one of these you have, let us direct from the degree of the Hyleg to the square aspect of the malefics and their opposition [signifying] death; and then let us look to see whether any benefic casts its own light on the place of the light of the malefic or not. But if there is any benefic Planet casting its own light upon the place of the light of the malefic, he will be freed [from death] after [suffering] pain.

After that, you will also direct it to the square aspect of another malefic and to its opposition; and the malefics give testimony when they are weakened in trine or sextile aspect. But what it would signify from the degrees of the Hyleg up to the *light* – that is to the *rays* of the malefic; [in which case,] we say that they will be years or months or days or hours, according to what the one that was ruling signified – whether they are years or months or days or hours. You will direct that division [of time] from the degree of the Hyleg up to the square aspect of the malefics or to their opposition, [as an indicator] for death.

A Question by a certain Duke who ruled Africa by order of the King, but with another Person opposing.

The Question of a certain Duke whom the king put in charge of Africa.[1] And there was then one who was in charge of Africa in opposition to them, and by those rebelling [against him] proper to be deposed. And the Duke asked whether or not what the king had preordained for him as the Duke of Africa would be useful for him, and what would be his future and the future of the one who ruled it,

---

[1] I have not been able to find a reference to a particular individual who was put in charge of Africa by the Caliph in 794 or 795. During the period 787 to 800 North Africa was dominated by various local tribal leaders, among whom was Idrîs (d. 793), who later established himself in Morocco. But in 800 Ibrâhîm ibn Aghlad (d. 811) was appointed to the government of the province of Africa (principally Egypt) by the Caliph Hârûn al-Rashîd (reigned 786-809). If Ibrahîm was the "certain Duke" of whom Mâshâ°allâh speaks, his opponent may have been some local chieftain in Egypt or even Idrîs II ibn Idrîs (d. 828), the ruler of Morocco, although he and Ibrâhîm are said to have ruled more or less independently.

by the will of God.

I looked at this Question by the will of God, and its Planets were just as I am saying to you. The ASC was Sagittarius 9 degrees. And the Sun in Sagittarius 8 degrees and 15 minutes; and Venus in Sagittarius 11 degrees and 31 minutes; and the Moon in Capricorn 22 degrees and 43 minutes; Saturn in Taurus 29 degrees and 54 minutes retrograde. And Jupiter in Virgo 20 degrees and 55 minutes; and Mars in Cancer 24 degrees and 40 minutes retrograde. And Mercury in Scorpio 29 degrees and 18 minutes retrograde, just as is shown in this figure.[1]

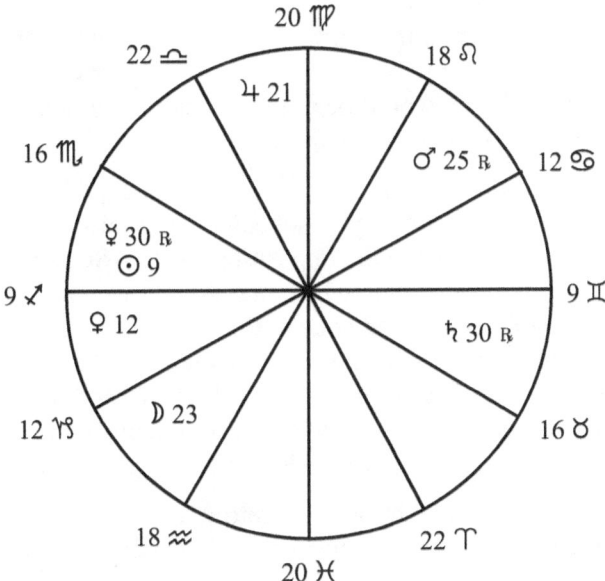

[1]The figure was presumably set for sunrise at Baghdad about 7 AM LAT (=6:53 AM LMT) on Monday 1 December 794. The planetary positions were calculated from tables based on a fixed zodiac. The house cuspal figures are those shown in the chart in the printed book and are (except for the MC and the ASC) of course not original.

And so, in this Question I looked at the ASC and its ruler, and the Planet from which the Moon is separated; and the ASC was Sagittarius, and the Sun and Venus were in it; and Jupiter the ruler of the ASC is direct in the MC, and it is one of the higher Planets, and it was aspecting both of its own domiciles and all the 4 angles, [while located] in a superior and higher place; with all the angles [and] the ruler of the Question in a more dignified place, namely the place of the exaltation of the ruler of the Question and his king-dom; and the Sun was being joined to Jupiter; and Venus [was be-ing joined to Jupiter] from his own domicile; and he was receiving them from his own domicile—a strong reception; and the Sun was receiving her by his own light; and testimonies were joined to him over good fortune, by the will of God; and Saturn signified the strength of the ruler of the Question over his enemy, and the firm-ness of his honor, and that he would get his kingdom, and that it would extend to that which was entrusted to him by his own em-peror; and that there would be nothing lacking that he would not get in his own hands, by the will of God.

After that I looked at the one who ruled Africa, who supported the rebels; and was contrary, disobedient, and must be set aside, from the *nadir*,[1] *i.e.* from the opposition to the ASC, and from its ruler; and from the Planet to which the Moon was joined at the *na-dir*, the sign of Gemini; and none of the 7 Planets was in it; and its ruler was Mercury, one of the inferior Planets; and it was retro-grade and cadent in the 12th sign from the ASC; and it was joined after its own direction to Saturn by opposition; but Saturn was also cadent in the 6th sign from the ASC, and was retrograde.

Therefore, Mercury, by its own retrogradation and position in its detriment,[2] and by its connection with a cadent and retrograde

---

[1] Reading *nadir* 'nadir' rather than *nabir*. The Arabic word is *nazîr*, which can mean 'opposite', so it is commonly used for the point opposite the zenith, i.e. the astronomical nadir. But Mâshâ²allâh uses it in the simple sense of 'opposite' any-thing. So for him the *nadir* of the ASC is the DSC. I have therefore italicized it to indicate its different sense in this text.

[2] Mâshâ²allâh is perhaps considering that Mercury is very close to Sagittarius, which is its detriment.

Planet, signified the annulment of those things that the enemy and opposing person had entered—that is, the annulment of his purpose, and the dissolution of his rulership; and in the 12th from the ASC, it signified his fall; and the fall of Saturn in the 12th from the *nadir*,[1] the debility and cadency of the enemy and adversary, namely strongly, and the disposition of that group, and the fall of its name or its memory; and the annulment of those that he equipped, and whom he had gathered together, and their building up, by the will of God.

After that I looked at the ruler of the Question and also at the Planet from which the Moon is separated. And the Moon was separating from Jupiter, who was the ruler of the ASC, and Jupiter was in the MC; and it is one of the higher Planets, having the higher place next after Saturn. And by the will of God, Jupiter signified through its elevation and the goodness of its place the strength of the ruler of the Question and the firmness of his honor and the attainment of his rulership and of those things that he asked about in connection with the honor; and namely about his dukedom, which his emperor and commander entrusted to him by the will of God.

Then I looked at the one who was being stirred up by rebels, and being set aside he was also disobedient, from the Planet to which the Moon was joined. And the Moon was also being joined to Mars; and Mars was cadent in his own fall and retrograde, i.e. in the 8th house from the ASC, which is the 2nd from the *nadir*; and it is the House of Auxiliaries, i.e of the soldiers of the one who was stirring up the rebels, and [the House of] his Wealth. The connection of the Moon and Mars, and the retrogradation of Mars, and his location in his fall, signified the dissolution of that work of the enemy and adversary; and his turning back from the purpose that he had set in motion and the loss of his honor, by the will of God.

And I also looked at the place of the Moon in the 2nd sign from the ASC, which is the Querent's House of Soldiers and Auxiliaries, and also the House of his Wealth. And the Moon is the

---

[1] That is, the 12th from the 7th, which is the 6th from the ASC.

significator of the enemy and adversary; [and she is herself] the significator of his soldiers and auxiliaries; and the Moon was joined to Mars by opposition; and each of them was receiving its own partner by a strong reception.

It therefore signified, by the will of God, the entrance of the Moon, who is the significator of the Auxiliaries of the enemy and adversary, into Capricorn, which is the House of the Auxiliaries of the ruler of the Question and the House of Wealth of the enemy adversary with the seeking of soldiers of the enemy adversary, the possession of wealth, namely, of the fulfillment of his own hope of acquiring wealth; and that they may receive part of those things that they had sought, by the will of God, and that they enter in obedience; and support of the ruler of the Querent.

After the acquisition of those things of which they were having hope, i.e. the gifts that they were hoping that they would be going to receive by the will of God, also, the place of the Moon in Capricorn and the place of Mars in Cancer signified, that they would not receive everything that they were hoping to receive, or just as they were thinking about it.

And the connection of the Moon to Mars by opposition signified that the soldiers of the adversary would be [engaged] in the seeking of wealth in the port; for that was their intention, and they were seeking that, by the will of God.

After that, I looked for the enemy adversary, what would be his future prospects, and about who would be succeeding him; therefore, I looked at Mercury who was the significator of the enemy—namely, I looked at the one to which he was being joined and who was being joined to him; and I found him to be joined to Saturn after his own direction by opposition, which is an aspect of contrariety and enmity; and Saturn was the ruler of the 2nd House of the Question and the ruler of the 3rd house of that same [chart], which are the places of his soldiers and the firmness of his auxiliaries; and there was no reception between them; this signified that the enemy himself would find some persons opposed to himself who would return themselves in turn and would ignore his word, i.e. his obedience from his brothers and soldiers, by the will of God.

After that, I looked at which one of them would have the victory and the acquisition of the kingdom from him—namely, from the rulers of their houses, because their significators were cadent from the angles. We should also look at those who were fighting against the enemy from Mercury, and his adversity from Saturn, and from the ruler of his domicile; and Saturn was cadent, retrograde, and the ruler of his domicile was Venus; and Venus was in the ascending angle, combust, and under the Sun beams. And her place in an angle in Sagittarius signified because it is a common sign the repetition of the battle by those who were adversaries of the enemy; namely, that would be adversarial to the enemy; they would increase the pressure on him by two times or more; and that would happen in the zeal of battle; and the combustion of Venus signified their killing and flight and their destruction, by the will of God.

After that, I looked at that same enemy adversary, to see what would be his strength and victory against those who were opposing him; and so, I looked at him from his own significator, and from the ruler of his house, and his significator was Mercury; and the ruler of his domicile was Mars; and Mars was in Cancer, his own fall, retrograde; and that was signifying weakness in initiating his work, by the will of God.

I also looked to see if Mars would be joined to any one that would strengthen him, or if any Planet would be joined to him that might aid him. And I found the Moon had joined herself [to him] from the exaltation of Mars; and each one of them was receiving his own partner by a strong reception. Therefore, this signified the victory of the enemy adversary over his own enemies, and that he would make them subject to himself, and he would receive whatever they were having of the kingdom in his own hands, by the will of God.

Then I looked at what would be [the situation] of the ruler of the Question and the opposing enemy, and how the ruler of the Question would get the kingdom, and whether he would have it by battle or by peace. I therefore looked at Jupiter, who was the significator of the ruler of the Question, and at Mercury, who was the significator of the opposing enemy, who was stirring up the rebels—from what part of the circle they were aspecting.

I found the one that was projecting its own light on its partner by a sextile aspect, namely one of peace and quiet and concord. And that signified that the attainment of the ruler of the Question had taken command of those things, and his exaltation over him would be by peace and by ease; and that it was the enemy who was stirring up the rebels; and there would also be security and peace, because Mercury was returning to Jupiter, and it was the lighter of the stars, and therefore it would be joined to it by the will of God.

INDEX OF PERSONS

BIBLIOGRAPHY

Abu ⁽Ali al-Khayyat
The Judgments of Nativities.
translated by James H. Holden
Tempe, Az.: A.F.A., Inc., 1988. paper 104 pp. diagrs
Tempe, Az.: A.F.A., Inc., 2009. paper 2nd. ed. xxviii,148 pp.
diagrs.

Dorotheus Sidonius
Carmen Astrologicum.
edited and the Arabic version translated
by David Pingree
Leipzig: B. G. Teubner Verlagsgesellschaft, 1976.

Firmicus Maternus, Julius
Matheseos Libri VIII
ed. by W. Kroll, F. Skutsch, and K. Ziegler
Leipzig: B. G. Teubner Verlagsgesellschaft, 1968. 2nd ed.

Lane-Poole, Stanley
The Mohammadan Dynasties.
New York: Frederick Ungar Publ. Co., 1965. repr of 1893 ed.

Leopold of Austria
Compilatio de astrorum scientia.
[Compilation of the Science of the Stars]
Augsburg: Erhard Ratdolt, 1489.

al-Nadîm
The Fihrist of al-Nadîm edited and translated
by Bayard Dodge
New York and London: Columbia University Press, 1970. 2
vols.

Ptolemy, Claudius
Tetrabiblos.
edited and translated by F. E. Robbins, Ph.D.
London: William Heinemann Ltd.;
Cambridge, Mass.: Harvard University Press, 1940. xxiv,466 pp.

Sahl ibn Bishr
The Introduction to the Science
of the Judgments of the Stars.
translated by James Herschel Holden
Tempe, Az.: A.F.A., Inc., 2008. paper xxii,214 pp.

MÂSHÂ'ALLÂH

THE BOOK OF NATIVITIES

Translated from the Twelfth Century Latin Version
by John of Seville

by

JAMES HERSCHEL HOLDEN, M.A.
Fellow of the American Federation of Astrologers

Contents

TRANSLATOR'S PREFACE

Mâshâ⟩allâh was the adopted Muslim name of the Jewish astrologer Mîshâ ibn Athrâ from Basra, Iraq, who converted to Islam and became one of the greatest Arabian[1] astrologers. He was born about 730 A.D. and lived until about 815. He was one of the astrological consultants employed by the Caliph al-Manṣûr (679-777) to make an election for the founding of the new city of Baghdad in 762.[2] Al-Nadîm[3] says this about Mâshâ⟩allâh: "He was a man of distinction and during his period the leading person for the science of judgments of the stars."

He was probably acquainted with the Greek astrologer Theophilus (d. 777), who seems to have been the first prominent Arabian astrologer. Theophilus wrote several books on astrology that survive in Greek versions, but the Arabic versions were unknown to the Twelfth Century Translators, who turned much Arabian astrology into Latin and sparked the recovery of astrology in Western Europe.

Mâshâ⟩allâh thus became the earliest Arabian astrologer whose works were known in the West. He wrote on a variety of subjects and was considered by both later Arabian astrologers and European astrologers to be a prime authority. His *Book on Nativities* is

---

[1]By *Arabian*, I mean all those, of whatever ethnic group, who wrote in the Arabic language.
[2]See my paper "The Foundation Chart of Baghdad" in *Today's Astrologer* Vol. 65, No. 3 (March 2, 2003): 9-10 & 29.
[3]From the priceless catalogue of Arabic literature as it existed at the end of the 10th century, *The Fihrist of al-Nadîm* edited and translated by Bayard Dodge (New York and London: Columbia University Press, 1970. 2 vols.), II, p. 650.

one of the earliest Arabian treatises currently available on the subject of nativities. His method of interpretation is that of the first century Greek astrologer Dorotheus Sidonius, as set forth in his *Pentateuch*. That book has not come down to us intact in the original Greek. However, there is an edition of the fragmentary Arabic translation and of the scattered citations of the book by later Greek astrologers.[1]

Dorotheus set forth a method of interpreting natal horoscopes that depends in the main on the triplicity rulers of the Light of the Time. Each triplicity has three rulers—a first ruler, a second ruler, and a third ruler. These can refer to the first third of a Native's life, the second third of his life, and the last third of his life. The triplicity rulers are these. For diurnal nativities, the rulers of Aries and its triplicity are the Sun, Jupiter, and Saturn; the rulers of the Taurus triplicity are Venus, the Moon, and Mars; the rulers of the Gemini triplicity are Saturn, Mercury, and Jupiter; and the rulers of the Cancer triplicity are Venus, Mars, and the Moon. For nocturnal nativities, the order of the first two rulers is reversed—for example, the nocturnal rulers of the Aries triplicity are Jupiter, the Sun, and Saturn.

Dorotheus also makes use of several Lots (or Parts as they are called today) and the rulers of the houses. Special attention is given to the ruler of the ASC.

Mâshâallâh adopts Dorotheus's techniques; and he also gives twelve natal horoscopes as examples. However, only three of these are from Dorotheus, and the other nine are from an unidentified Greek source of perhaps the sixth century that contained a number of charts from the fifth century. One of the latter is from a treatise by the early sixth century astrologer Rhetorius the Egyptian; and two others have not been possible to date with any certainty. Evidently some now lost Greek MS containing those charts was available (in Arabic translation) to Mâshâallâh.

---

[1]Dorotheus Sidonius, *Carmen Astrologicum*, edited and the Arabic translated by David Pingree (Leipzig: B. G. Teubner Verlagsgesellschaft, 1976).

The reader may wonder why Mâshâ⁾allâh used old Greek charts as examples rather than some Arabic ones from his own time. I addressed that question previously as follows:

> "Mâshâ⁾allâh was one of the first astrologers who wrote in Arabic. Not many had practiced the art in the Caliphate before him. It seems likely that he had no Notable Nativities of the 8th century from which to take examples. And I think he would not have dared to use the charts of prominent Muslims either living or of recent memory. Thus, it is possible that he used the old Greek charts out of necessity."[1]

I had previously published a translation of Mâshâ⁾allâh's *Book of Nativities* in Appendix 2 of my translation of his pupil Abû ⁽Alî's book *The Judgments of Nativities*, and in Chapter 7 of that book he discusses the twelve charts given by Mâshâ⁾allâh. His charts differ in details from the charts at the end of Pingree's edition of Mâshâ⁾allâh's *Book of Nativities* that is contained in Appendix 3 of his and E. S. Kennedy's book *The Astrological History of Mâshâ⁾allâh* (Cambridge, Mass.: Harvard University Press, 1971).

The present translation is a slightly revised version of my earlier translation, but I have added Mâshâ⁾allâh's interpretations of the twelve charts from Pingree's edition. Abû ⁽Alî's interpretations of the twelve charts are more extensive and often better—for them, see my translation of his book, *The Judgments of Nativities*, which also contains my notes on the individual charts as they are shown in that book.

In Pingree's edition, Charts 1 and 2 have cuspal degrees calculated according to the Alchabitius system for a Latitude of 43 N. Since Charts 1 and 2 were taken originally from Dorotheus, the cuspal degrees are not authentic and were presumably added by

---

[1]Abu ⁽Ali al-Khayyat, *The Judgments of Nativities* translated by James H. Holden (Tempe, Az.: A.F.A., Inc., 1988), p. 79; repr. 2008, p. 111.

the scribe of MS Parisinus graecus 2506 (early 14th century). or perhaps by the author of his exemplar. The Alchabitius system had not yet been invented in the first century, and Dorotheus only gives the rising sign (no ASC degree) for his charts, so he probably used the Sign-House system. And the Latitude of Sidon is 33N34. But I have drawn those charts here with the cuspal numbers shown in Pingree's edition.

Pingree's edition of Charts 8-12 also has a full set of Alchabitius house cusps. But they too are set for a Latitude of 43 N, so they cannot have been calculated by Mâshâ'allâh, who wrote in Baghdad whose Latitude is 33N14. They were probably added by the scribe as mentioned above. Apparently he kept the ASC sign mentioned in the text, but made an arbitrary choice of ASC degree, and from that he determined the MC and the other house cusps.

Chart 10 is from Rhetorius, who in one of his minor treatises gave the ASC as 25 Taurus 16 and the MC as 3 Aquarius 37 (it should have been 2 Aquarius 41). Rhetorius then assumed that the cusp of the ASC was 5 degrees less, or 20 Taurus 16, and proceeded to calculate what we call Alchabitius cusps for the intermediate houses.[1] And the Latitude was that which Ptolemy called the 5th Clime or 40N56., which was appropriate for Constantinople.

In Pingree's edition, Chart 10 has 11 Taurus rising, which is not correct. Abû Alî kept the correct ASC but did not give any of the other cusps. However, to be consistent, I have shown the chart as Pingree gives it. The reader may wish to compare it with the chart that is given in Abû ʿAlî al-Khayyât's book *The Judgments of Nativities.*[2] And O. Neugebauer and H. B. Van Hoesen also discuss Rhetorius's version of the chart in their book, *Greek Horoscopes* (Philadelphia: American Philosophical Society, 1959.)

---

[1]This is the earliest known example of the calculation of Alchabitius cusps, which are a minor variant of Porphyry cusps.

[2]See Abu ʿAli al-Khayyat, *The Judgments of Nativities.* ʿAlî, who lived in the first half of the 9th century, was a pupil of Mâshâ'allâh and presumably had copies of Mâshâ'allâh's books.

MÂSHÂʾALLÂH
THE BOOK OF NATIVITIES

Chapter 1. *Whether the child will [live to] be weaned or not.*

Mâshâʾllâh said that among all the books of astrology there is not one that is found to be more useful than *The Book of Nativities*, nor one so good in judgments. He who is versed in it will find knowledge and wisdom in it, and he will delight in its practical knowledge.

First, it should be known whether the child will [live to] be weaned or not. And you will know this from the ASC, namely from the rulers of its triplicity, and from the rulers of the domicile of the Sun if the Nativity is diurnal, or from the rulers of the domicile of the Moon if it is nocturnal; and from the ruler of the New Moon or the ruler of the Full Moon if he was born after the New Moon or the Full Moon.

And if it is the New Moon or the full Moon, you will look at the rulers of its triplicity. And in addition, you will look at Jupiter and Venus. And if the Nativity is diurnal, you will look at the diurnal Planets; and if it is nocturnal, at the nocturnal Planets.

And you will begin to look at the [first] ruler of the triplicity of the first house, i.e. the ASC, and at the second ruler, and at the third ruler; and these are the rulers of the triplicity of the first [house]. And if they are free [from any aspect of] the malefics, namely in the ASC, or in the 10th house or in the 11th or in the 5th, the Native will live.

But if they are cadent from the angles and are malefics, you will look at the rulers of the triplicity of the Sun's domicile if it is a diurnal Nativity. But if it is a nocturnal Nativity, you will look at the rulers of the triplicity of the Moon's domicile. And if they are in a good house and safe from [any aspect of] the malefics, the Native will live.

But if they are in evil houses and are malefics, you will look at the rulers of the triplicity of the domicile of the Part of Fortune. And if they are in a good house and free from [any aspect of] the malefics, the Native will live.

But if it is a diurnal Nativity, you will look at the Part of Fortune; and if it is a nocturnal Nativity, you will look at the Moon. And if it is in an evil house, you will look at the rulers of the triplicity of the domicile of the conjunction of the Sun and the Moon if the Nativity was after the New Moon. Or you will look at the rulers of the triplicity of the domicile of the Full Moon if the Nativity was after the Full Moon. And if they are angular and free from [any aspect of] the malefics, the Native will live.

But if they are malefics and impedited, then look at Jupiter, which is a helper in Nativities. And if it is in an angle or in a succedent of an angle and free from [any aspect of] the malefics, he will live. But if it is in an evil house and impedited by a malefic, you will look at Venus; and if it is in an angle or in a succedent of an angle and free from [any aspect of] the malefics, he will live.

But if it is in an evil house and impedited by the malefics,[1] you will look at the Moon. And if it is in the ASC or the 10th house, and free from [any aspect of] the evil Planets, [and] it is joined to a diurnal star if the Nativity is diurnal, or joined to a nocturnal star if the Nativity is nocturnal, and it is free from [any aspect of] the malefics, he will live. But if it is evilly placed, you will look at the *Almuten*.[2]

---

[1] Literally, 'by afflicted [Planets]', but I think he means the evil Planets.

[2] *Almuten* is a corruption of the Arabic word *al-mubtazz*, a derivative of the verb *bazza* 'to triumph' or 'to be victorious over someone'. So *al-mubtazz* is the equivalent of the classical Greek word *epikratêtôr* 'ruler', used in the sense of the principal ruler.

And you will know from the rulers of the triplicity of the ASC, and if it is a diurnal Nativity, from the rulers of the triplicity of the Sun; and if it is a nocturnal Nativity, from the rulers of the domicile of the conjunction of the Sun and the Moon if the Nativity is after the New Moon; or by the rulers of the triplicity of the domicile of the Full Moon if the Nativity is before the New Moon. And if they are in angles or in the succedents of the angles and free from [any aspect of] the malefics, he will live. But if they are in evil houses and impeded, he will die.

Then, you will look at the planet that is *Almuten*, and the one to which it communicates its disposition, and how many degrees are between them. And if it is in a fixed sign, you will give one year to each degree; and if it is in a common sign, you will give a month to each degree; and if it is in a mobile sign, you will give a day to each degree. But if the *Almuten* is cadent, and an evil planet is in the ASC, and the Moon is joined to an evil Planet, he will live as much time as there are degrees. That is, if the receiver of the disposition is impeded and in a fixed sign, they will be years; and if in a common sign, months; and if in a mobile sign, days.

Then, look at the degrees of the Sun or the Moon. If either of them aspects the *Almuten* by square or conjoins it in the same domicile or opposes it, it will be evil, unless the degrees of *Athazer* are there.[1] And, if any of the degrees of *Athazer* are there, he will live as many years or months or days (as was said above) as there are degrees.[2] But if the *Almuten* is joined to a malefic by the square or opposition aspect, and no benefic aspects it, the newborn will

---

[1] The word *Athazer* is from the Arabic *al-tasyirat* 'staring-points' used to translate the Greek *aphetês* 'starter'. It designates a series of elongations of the Moon from the Sun that were considered to be significant in certain cases. Wright gives the list: 0°, 12°, 45°, 90°, 135°, 168°, 180°, 192°, 225°, 270°, 315°, and 348° (Al-Bîrûnî, *The Book of Instruction*, Sect. 254, n.1.). These numbers are simply the usual Moon phases (conjunction, 1st quarter, etc.) along with half-phases or octants (half-way between the New Moon and the 1st quarter, etc.). To these are added the 12° points on either side of the conjunction, which mark the approximate points where the Moon becomes visible or invisible. And, for the sake of symmetry, 12° points on either side of the opposition.

[2] That is, if the number of degrees between the significators coincides with one of the *Athazer* numbers, he will live that number of years, months, or days.

scarcely live. But if the Moon is configured between two malefics, and one of them is in the ASC, and the other is in the 7th, and the Moon is badly [situated] in an angle, he will die.

But [if] the rulers of the triplicity of the ASC, or the rulers of the triplicity of the Sun's domicile, and the rulers of the Part of Fortune's domicile, and the rulers of the triplicity of the New Moon or the Full Moon, are impedited or cadent; and any Planet is in [a position of] strength, he will have serious illnesses. And if the rulers of the triplicity of the ASC are cadent, he will die. And it will be worse if one of the aforesaid is Saturn in a nocturnal Nativity or Mars in a diurnal Nativity, namely in one of the angles.

But if the Moon is received and the ruler of the ASC is in a good house, he will live, and he will be honored, and he will have many brothers. But if there is no reception, it indicates poverty.

If the Part of Fortune is with the Moon, and it aspects Venus in a nocturnal Nativity or Jupiter in a diurnal Nativity, it indicates high position and life, just as when the Part of Fortune is in a good house.

Every planet that is a significator and is oriental in a diurnal Nativity and in a masculine sign, or is occidental in a nocturnal Nativity and in a feminine sign, will have good strength, and its testimony will be good; and it indicates high status for the Native.

But if the ruler of the ASC or the Moon is in an evil [house], and the ruler of the domicile of the Moon is in an angle, it indicates death.

And when you know that the Native will not live long, you will make *Athazer* from the ASC degree up to the evil Planet that impedites, and you will give to each sign one month. But if the Native makes it through these months, he will live as many years as the months that were predicted.

Then, look at the ruler of the 5th house. If it is in a good house, the prediction must be judged good; if it is in an evil [house], it will narrow his own soul in poverty.

When there is a Hyleg in the Nativity and when there is Not.

Chapter 2. *The Hyleg is the Knowledge of Life: When the Nativity of the Child indicates Life.*

And when you want to know this, select[1] the Sun as Hyleg[2] in a diurnal Nativity. And if it is in an angle or in a succedent of an angle and in a masculine sign or in a masculine quarter—i.e., from the 1st house to the MC[3]—and the ruler of the domicile aspects it, or the ruler of the terms, or the ruler of the exaltation, or the ruler of the triplicity or of the face, it will be the Hyleg. And if none of these aspects it, it will not be the Hyleg.

Then, you will look at the Moon. And if it is in an angle or in a succedent of an angle, and in a feminine sign or in a feminine quarter, and it is aspect just as I said in the case of the Sun, you will accept it as the Hyleg.

But if the Sun or the Moon is not the Hyleg, you will look at the ruler of the domicile of the New Moon or the Full Moon. If it is not the Hyleg, you will look at the ruler of the domicile of the Part of Fortune. And if you don't find it to be the Hyleg, you will put the ASC degree for the Hyleg if the ruler of the ASC aspects the ASC. But if all the aforesaid fail, there will be no Hyleg.

The Indication of Time from the *Alcochoden*.

Chapter 3. *The Alcochoden, through which is known the Computation [of the Length] of Life.*

And when the Hyleg has been found, you will look at the *Alcochoden*.[4] And you will look at the Hyleg and the ruler of its

---

[1] Reading *elige* 'select' instead of *dirige* 'direct'.

[2] Hyleg is from the Arabic word *al-hîlâj* from the Persian word *hîlâk* 'letting loose' which was the equivalent of the classical Greek word *aphetês* 'the aphetic place (lit. 'starter'). It was the significator of the life of the Native according to Ptolemy, *Tetrabiblos*, iii. 10.

[3] The printed text has '7th house forwards', but the 7th house is in a feminine quarter.

[4] Variously spelled in Latin, it is from the Arabic *al-kadkhudâh*, which is from a

terms, and the ruler of its triplicity, and the ruler of its domicile, and the ruler of its exaltation, and the ruler of its face. And the one of these that aspects the Hyleg will be the *Alcochoden*. But if one or two or three of the planets aspects the Hyleg, the planet that is the most dignified will be the *Alcochoden*.

You may know that when the Sun is in Aries or Leo, it will be the Hyleg and the *Alcochoden*.[1] Similarly, if the Moon is in Taurus or in Cancer, it will be the Hyleg and the *Alcochoden* whether they aspect it or not, and similarly with the Sun.

And when you have found the *Alcochoden*, look at it. If it is in an angle[2] or in its own domicile or in its own exaltation of triplicity, safe from any impediment, namely from retrogradation or from combustion by the Sun, you will give it the major years of the Planet. And if it is in a succedent of an angle, and safe from [any aspect of] the malefics, you will give it the middle years. But if it is in a cadent from an angle, and has no dignity there, you will give it the minor years.

And you may know that an augment of the years of a Planet, or a diminution of them does not take place except through the strength of the planet or through its debility. But if the Planet is oriental and in good state, you will give the greater years. And if it is not oriental, and it has an evil aspect with one [of the Planets], you will give it the minor years. And if it is occidental, and has an evil aspect with one [of the Planets], and is retrograde, you will give it as many weeks as its minor years. And if it is in an evil house in which it cannot be worse when retrograde [and is aspected by one] of the lighter Planets, you will give it as many days as are the minor years of the Planet.

And you may know that when the Head of the Dragon is in the same sign as the planet that is *Almuten*, less than 12 degrees either

---

Persian word used to translate the Greek *oikodespotês* 'house-ruler', often used to signify the 'ruler of the nativity'. Here it corresponds to the "giver of years."

[1]The MS has *erit alcoden erit yles alcoden*, for which read *erit yles et alcoden*.

[2]The MS has *ex gradibus* 'of degrees' after 'angle' by mistake.

before or after, it adds a fourth part of the years of the Planet that is *Almuten*; and if it is closer in degrees, it will be more effective. But if the Tail of the Dragon is there, it takes away a fourth part of the years. And if it is in [partile] conjunction with the Sun or the Moon, it takes away nothing. But if the Sun is the *Alcochoden* and is some distance away from it, it takes away from its years. Ptolemy said, the Head with the benefics adds good fortune, and the Tail takes away from the years.[1] But if the Head or the Tail is with the Sun or the Moon, the strength [of the Nodes] will appear for either good or evil, and more strongly in the case of the Moon.

But if Jupiter is in the ASC with Venus, each one of these adds its own minor years in the Nativity, unless the malefics impedite them, and unless the Moon is similarly in a bad state. But if one of the aforesaid benefics, viz. Jupiter and Venus, is the ruler of the House of Death, and is in the ASC, the newborn will die before it lives.

How Many Years the Planets Add to the *Alcochoden*.

Chapter 4. *[How] to Know What the Planets Add or Subtract.*

And when you know how many years you ought to put for the *Alcochoden*, and you want to know how many are taken away or added, look at the *Alcochoden*. If there is a benefic with it, and it aspects it by sextile or any other good aspect, and if it is in a good house, it will increase the minor years of that benefic. But if the benefics that aspect the *Alcochoden* are weak, in place of the minor *years*, you will give the same [number of] *months*. And if the benefic that aspects the *Alcochoden* is retrograde, and a malefic impedites it, there will be *days* in the same number as the minor *years*.

But if a malefic is with the *Alcochoden*, and that star will be the receiver of the degree of the *Alcochoden*, and they aspect each other by square aspect or by opposition, and they have a conjunc-

---

[1]Not in the *Tetrabiblos* or in pseudo-Ptolemy's *Centiloquy*. Perhaps in one of the spurious works attributed to Ptolemy.

tion with the ruler of the House of Death, there will be *hours* in the same number as the minor *years* of the *Alcochoden*. But if Mercury is in a good house and aspects the *Alcochoden* with a good aspect, its minor years will be an increment for it. And if it is the converse, it will be reduced by the number of [Mercury's] minor years. And the strongest of the planetary aspects with the *Alcochoden* is the aspect of Mars. But if you want to know the [time of] death with certainty, look at the malefic that impedites the *Alcochoden*; and when the *Alcochoden* comes to those degrees [by direction], he will die.

Whose Will is the Native's.

Chapter 5. *To Know the Will of the Native.*

Look at the ruler of the ASC and at Mercury, which indicates the speech of the Native; and if it is strong and in a mobile sign, it indicates that he has good speech and is honored and is fearing God.; and if it is in a common sign, it indicates that he has little wisdom and is irascible, and that he scarcely trusts the advice of others; and if it is in a fixed sign, it indicates that he will be honored, and that through his truth and goodness and advice in his own life, and in every way his advice will be very true, and it will free advice impeded by hindrances.

And if they are oriental and in angles or in the succedents of angles, it indicates a good and sharp type of intellect, and whatever he wants to do, he will do without any hindrance. And if they are occidental and cadent from the angles, it indicates that he has a malevolent heart, and that he associates with low persons, and that he is too irascible. And everything that has just been said is from the ruler of the ASC and the Moon; and if they are in a good house, say it is good; but if it is the other way around, [say that it is bad]. And each star will obtain rulership over [some part of] the human body.

But if the ruler of the ASC is the Sun, and it is in a good house free from the malefics, it indicates high position and honor and rulership; but if it is debilitated and in a cadent house, it indicates that he has a spirit with both little strength and little acquisition of wealth.

But if the Moon is the ruler of the ASC and in a good house free from the malefics, it indicates that he is honest and truthful; and if it is in an evil house, it shows that he is not truthful, but sad, and from his own mouth there will proceed [falsehoods][1] for which his body will be flogged and beaten.

If Saturn is the ruler of the ASC, and it is in a good house free from the malefics, it indicates that he is honored and popular and vigorous in speech, and apt, and prudent in advice; and if it is in an evil house, it indicates that he is sad and mournful and a deceiver.

If Jupiter is the ruler of the ASC and in a good house and free from the malefics, it indicates loftiness and honor and a good spirit; and if it is in an evil house, it indicates that he is untruthful and stingy.

If Mars is the ruler of the ASC and free from the malefics, it indicates that he is extravagant, and he will be strong in heart; and if it is in an evil house, it indicates that he is *alhagem*,[2] and he will be a spiller of blood or an executioner.

If Venus is the ruler of the ASC and in a good house, it indicates that he is handsome and of low degree; and if it is in an evil house, it indicates that he is eager; and if it is [the Nativity of] a woman, it indicates that she is a whore.

If Mercury is the ruler of the ASC and free from the malefics, it indicates that he is wise and a physician; and if it is the ruler of the ASC and joined to Saturn, it indicates that he is a stammerer, and a good physician in strong things, and he is voluptuous or a sodomite; and if it is joined with Jupiter, it indicates that he is good and wise, and that he will obtain a position of rulership; but if it is joined to Mars or in aspect with it, it indicates that he is a king or a

---

[1]The Latin text has *a lacuna* here. I have conjectured the word 'falsehoods' to fill it.
[2]I cannot identify this Arabic word.

royal secretary; and if it is joined to Venus, it indicates that he delights in wisdom and judgments, and that he will be dishonest in law, standing out in strength, either in his infirmity, or in haughtiness of mind, or in the loss of his knowledge.

You will know from the terms of the signs about their strength or weakness, just as I have taught in *The Book on the Nine Parts by Mâshâ'allâh*, and as it is written in Sahl [for] Alichel,[1] and Alicberz,[2] etc.

Then for the children of kings, you will look at the ASC degree; if there is any hot star at the aforesaid degree or in the MC, and the ASC is in a bright degree, or if the Sun is there in a diurnal Nativity or the Moon in a nocturnal Nativity, and the Native is born from the offspring of kings, it shows him to be under the power of the king, and he will be elevated in rank. But if it is a diurnal Nativity and the Sun is in Aries or the Moon is in its exaltation in a nocturnal Nativity, and it is in the MC or in the ASC degree, and there will be ascending one of those signs that indicates kings, and the ruler of the ASC is in a good house, it is an indication for a kingdom and for high rank.

But if the two Lights are joined to the ruler of the ASC in its own exaltation, it shows him to have a strong kingdom. But if the ruler of the ASC is joined with the ruler of the 10th house, and they are oriental, and it is in its own exaltation, he will be a most powerful king.

But if many stars are joined with Jupiter in the MC or in his exaltation, it indicates that he is an emperor; and every star that is *Almuten*, and is [located] as just said, will indicate very high rank for him.

But if the ruler of the triplicity of the ASC is joined with the

---

[1]*Alichel* is from the Arabic *al-iqbâl* 'progress'. This and the following Arabic word are mentioned and discussed in Sahl ibn Bishr, *The Introduction to the Science of the Judgments of the Stars* (Tempe, Az.: A.F.A., Inc., 2008), Book 1 "Introduction."

[2]*Alicberz* is from the Arabic *al-idbâr* 'deterioration'.

ruler of the ASC in the MC and is oriental, it designates him to be a king.

Work with the diurnal stars with the Sun, and with the nocturnal stars with the Moon. And if the Sun is in his own domicile, or in an angle, or in his joy, and the stars aspect each other mutually, it designates him to be a king.

The Good Fortune and Bad Fortune of the Native.

Chapter 6. *To know the Good Fortunes and Misfortunes of the Native [as shown] in his own Nativity.*

You will look at the rulers of the triplicity of the appropriate Light—in a diurnal Nativity, the Sun; and in a nocturnal one, the Moon. And if they are in an angle and free from the malefics, it indicates good fortune for the Native for all the days of his life. And if the first ruler of the triplicity is in the ASC from the 1st degree to the 15th, he will ascend to great wealth; and when it is more closely related to the degrees in the angle, it will be more useful for him. But if it is in the 2nd sign[1] from the 1st degree up to the 15th, . . .[2] But if the first ruler of the triplicity is in a good house, it will be good for him in the first time of his life; and if the second ruler of the triplicity is in a good house, it will be good for him in the second time of his life; and if the third ruler of the triplicity is in a good house, it will be good for him in the third time of his life; and if it is the other way around, it will be the reverse.[3]

But if a ruler of the triplicity of the Light [of the Time] is cadent and in an evil house, it indicates that he will have poverty, namely in that part of his life which is the first, the second, or the third. But if the rulers of the triplicity of the Light [of the Time] are in evil houses, and there are benefics in the angles, and the ASC aspects them, and they are not impeded, it indicates that he has good for-

---

[1]That is, the 2nd house! Mâshâ᾽allâh was speaking of the Sign-house system of house division.

[2]The conclusion is missing in the Latin.

[3]That is, if the three rulers are in evil houses, it will be bad for the Native in those times of his life.

tune. And if the Lights are not impedited, it will be better for him.

But if the ruler of the ASC and the Moon are in angles and free from the malefics, they indicate that he has wealth, and more so if they are received; but if the ruler of the ASC is joined to any one of the Lights in its own domicile or in its exaltation, or if the Lights join themselves to the ruler of the ASC, it indicates that he will excel in wealth.

And if the Part of Fortune and its ruler are in an angle, namely in the east and aspect the ASC, it indicates that he is extremely wealthy; and if they are in cadent and in bad places, it indicates that he has loss, and even worse unless the rulers of the triplicity of the ASC aspect the ASC. But if they are in the cadents of the angles and they are joined with benefics in the angles, it indicates that he has more good than loss. When the ruler of the ASC is cadent and in its own fall and joined with a Planet that is in its own exaltation or in its own domicile, it indicates that he has good after loss.

[The End]

Hereafter, in his edition of the *Book of Nativities*,[1] Pingree inserts twelve natal horoscopes, some of them taken from Dorotheus's *Pentateuch* (Leipzig: B.G. Teubner, 1976); the others are taken from an unknown Greek source of the 5th or 6th century. And yet, as Pingree says, Mâshâ'allâh writes as if he himself had cast them and interpreted them.

All of these charts are also given by Mâshâ'allâh's pupil Abû ⟨Alî al-Khayyât in his book *The Judgments of Nativities* (Tempe, Az.: A.F.A., Inc., 1988). However, some of the charts at the end of Mâshâ'allâh's *Book of Nativities* have ASC degrees that differ from those in Abû ⟨Alî's book, and they also have MC's and intermediate cuspal figures. However, these cannot have been part of Mâshâ'allâh's text, because they are Alchabitius cusps set for a geographic Latitude of about 43 N. (But Chart 10 was accurately

---

[1]Kennedy, E. S. and David Pingree, *The Astrological History of Mâshâ'allâh* (Cambridge, Mass.: Harvard University Press, 1971).

calculated by Rhetorius.)

In Appendix 1, I have therefore reproduced the charts as they appeared in Pingree's edition., but I have redrawn them in the round form and appended notes.

APPENDIX.

TWELVE NATAL HOROSCOPES.

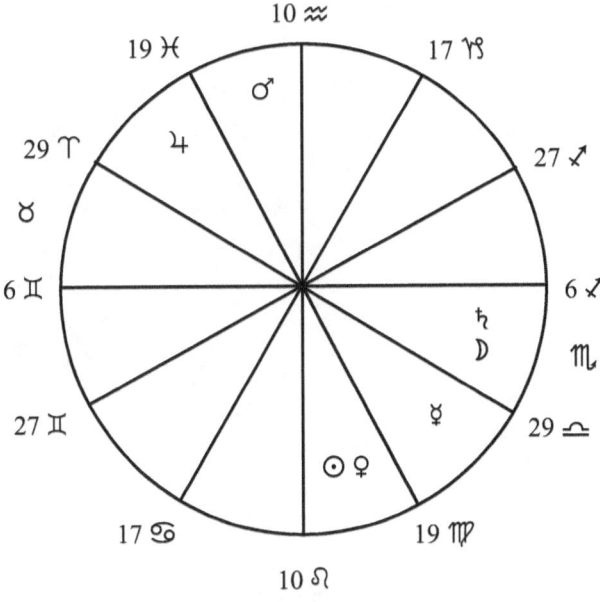

Chart 1.

I looked at the fortune of this Native from the rulers of the Moon's triplicity because the Nativity was nocturnal. And the first ruler of the triplicity was Mars, Venus was the second ruler, and the Moon was the third ruler of the triplicity. I judged him to be impoverished, and at the time that I saw him [he was] a beggar. And he died in misery and poverty. And all of that is shown in this figure.

This chart is from Dorotheus's *Pentateuch*, Book 1, where it was set for 2 or 3 August 43 A.D. at about 1 A.M. and considered in Sign-House mode. As shown above, the medieval copyist added Alchabitius house cusps for 43N.

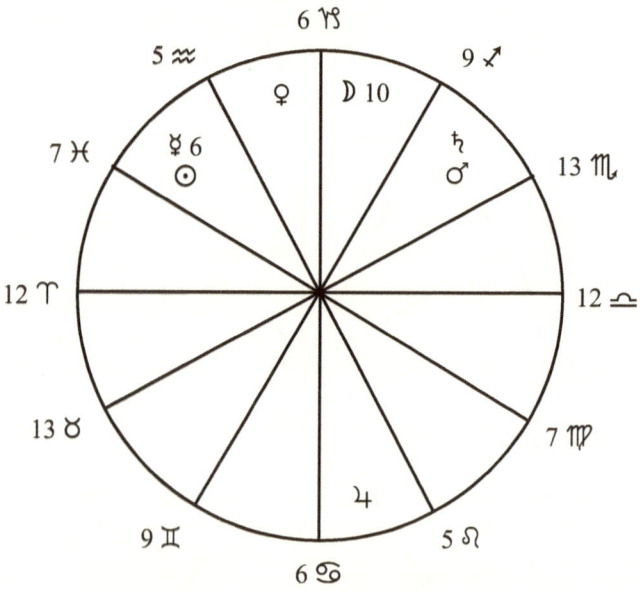

Chart 2.

I looked at the fortune of this Native from the rulers of the Sun's triplicity because it was a diurnal Nativity. And the [first] ruler of the triplicity was Saturn, and the second ruler was Mercury, and it was almost in an angle; and one of them was in the DSC and the other in the MC. Then I judged that he would have goodness and much stamina. And so it was always good.

Note that in his commentary Mâshâ⁾allâh puts both Saturn and Mercury in the wrong houses. Abû ⁽Alî corrects this and says "…both of them are in succedents…"

Pingree dates this chart to 29 January 425 and ascribes it to an unknown Greek source. It has Alchabitius cusps set for latitude 43N. They were probably not original.

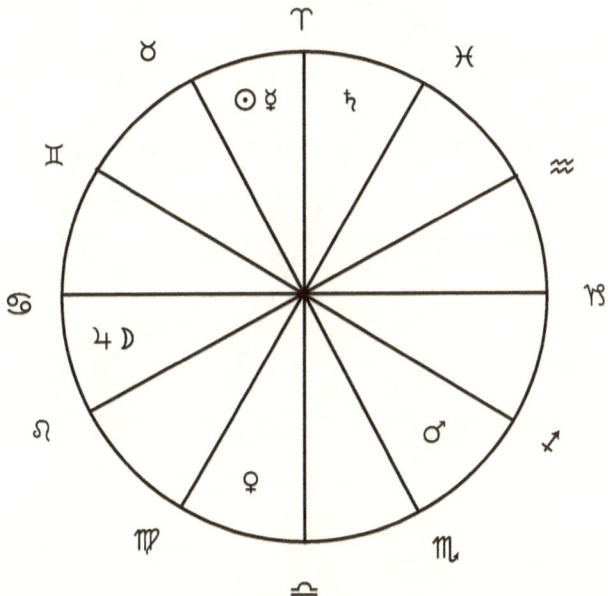

Chart 3.

I looked at the fortune of the Native from the rulers of the Sun's triplicity. And the first ruler of the triplicity is the Sun, and the second ruler is Jupiter, and the third ruler is Saturn. And I found these in angles and in their own exaltations. It was indicating that he would have good fortune and an elevated position. And Saturn did not harm him because it was in a domicile of Jupiter and was aspecting it by a good aspect.

This chart is from the *Pentateuch*, Book 1, where it is set for 29 or 30 March 22 A.D. at about 11 A.M. The Sun and Jupiter are in angles, but Saturn is not. Abû ʿAlî states it more correctly "...both [the Sun and Jupiter] are in angles and in their own exaltations..."

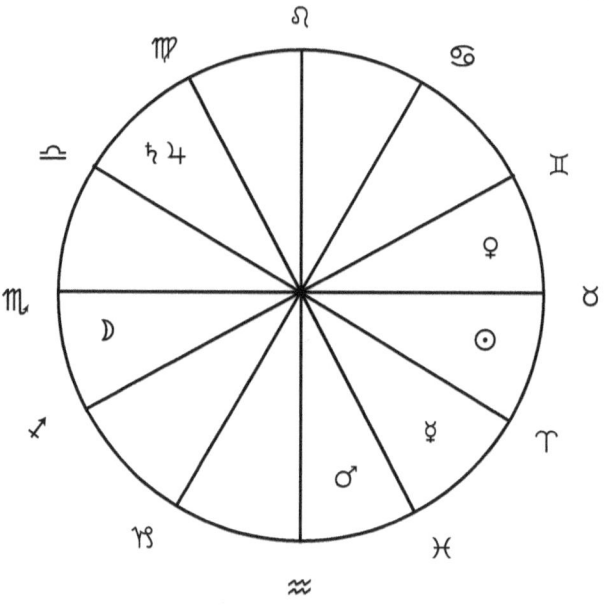

Chart 4.

I looked at his fortune from the rulers of the Moon's triplicity. And the first ruler of the triplicity is Mars, the second ruler is Venus, and the third ruler is the Moon. And I found these in angles. And therefore I judged that he would ascend into a very high place until he would acquire a golden crown. And so it was.

This chart is from the *Pentateuch*, Book 1, where it is set for 1 or 2 April 36 A.D. at about 7 P.M.

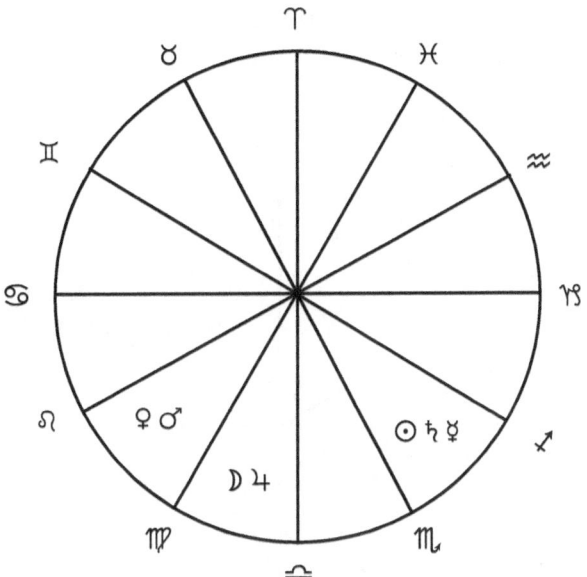

Chart 5.

I looked at the fortune of this Native from the rulers of the Moon's triplicity, which are Mercury first, Saturn second, and Jupiter third. And these were cadent. I judged for him misery and poverty. And so it was.

This chart is from an unknown Greek source. Mâshâʾallâh puts the Moon and Jupiter in Virgo, but Abû ʿAlî puts them in Gemini. Venus cannot be in Leo when the Sun is in Scorpio, so that is obviously wrong. On 14 Nov 70 Venus was in Scorpio and Mercury in Sagittarius, but the other planets were as shown in the chart.

With the Moon and Jupiter in Gemini as Abû ʿAlî has it, Pingree dates the chart to 9 Nov 542 [at about 9 P.M.], but 10 Nov and 11 Nov would be equally possible. All those dates put Venus in Capricorn

However, the commentaries of both Mâshâʾallâh and Abû ʿAlî

say that Mercury and Saturn are cadent; and Abû ʿAlî also says that Jupiter is in the 11th house. None of which agrees with either version of the chart. It would therefore seem best to call this chart corrupt and undateable.

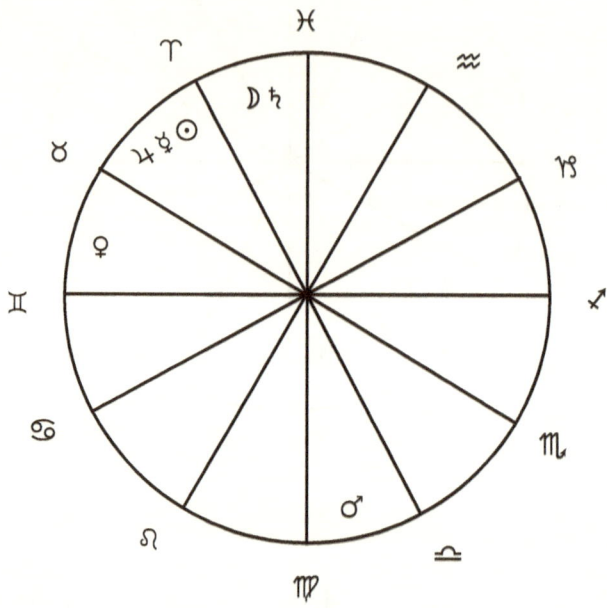

Chart 6.

I looked at the fortune of this Native from the rulers of the Sun's triplicity, the first of which is the Sun, the second ruler is Jupiter, and the third is Saturn. And I found these in angles. I judged that he would have high position and eminence and honor for all the days of his life. And so it was.

This chart is probably from the unknown Greek source. Pingree dated it to 24 March 434 A.D. [at about 10 A.M.], but 25 March 434 is equally possible.

However, on those dates Mercury was in Pisces, Mars was in

Leo, and Saturn was at the end of Aquarius according to Ptolemy's Tables. Mâshâ'allâh says that all the triplicity rulers were angular, but if we accept the chart as drawn, only Saturn was angular. However, in Abû ʿAlî's chart, the Sun is also angular in Pisces.

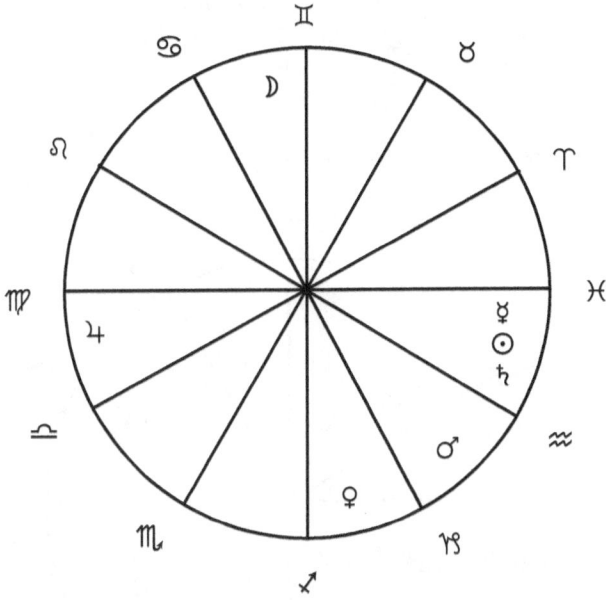

Chart 7.

I looked at the rulers of the Moon's triplicity, the first of which is Mercury, the second ruler is Saturn, and the third ruler is Jupiter. And I found these to be cadent from the angles and in evil houses. I judged him to be miserable and a beggar.

This chart is probably from the unknown Greek source. Pingree dates it to 19 January 403 A.D. [at about 7 P.M.]. But Mars was in Aquarius, not in Capricorn; and Venus was in Capricorn, not in Sagittarius. And actually, Jupiter was not cadent. Abû ʿAlî thought better of this chart. He says:

"…the first ruler of the triplicity was Mercury, the second Saturn, both cadent, which signified poverty and a bad condition for this Native, and so in fact it happened that this man was of narrow means, abounding in nothing other than sweat and hard work. But because Jupiter and Venus were in angles, they signified bodily health and good rearing, and sustenance from kings and princes and from many friends."

But his two significations seem to be almost contradictory.

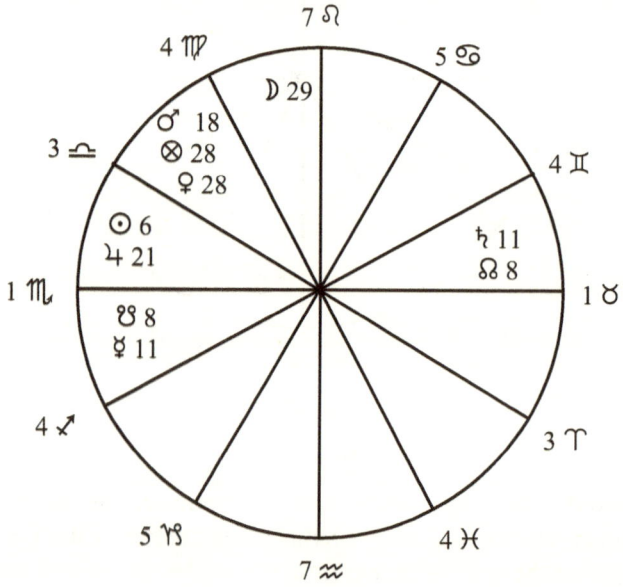

Chart 8.

I looked at the fortune of this Native from the rulers of the Sun's triplicity, of which the first was Saturn, the second Mercury, and the third Jupiter. I found these [Saturn and Mercury] aspecting [each other] by opposition. And Mercury was joined with Cauda, and Saturn with Caput. And Jupiter is cadent, and the Part of Fortune is with Mars, and the ruler of the Part of Fortune is joined with Cauda, and Saturn was in opposition. Then we judged that he would be very foolish and miserable. And all this is plain in this figure.

This chart is probably from the unknown Greek source. It is set for 19 October 439 at about 7 A.M. LAT. I have shown the house cusps as they are in Mâshâ°allâh's chart. They are Alchabitius cusps for Latitude 43N.

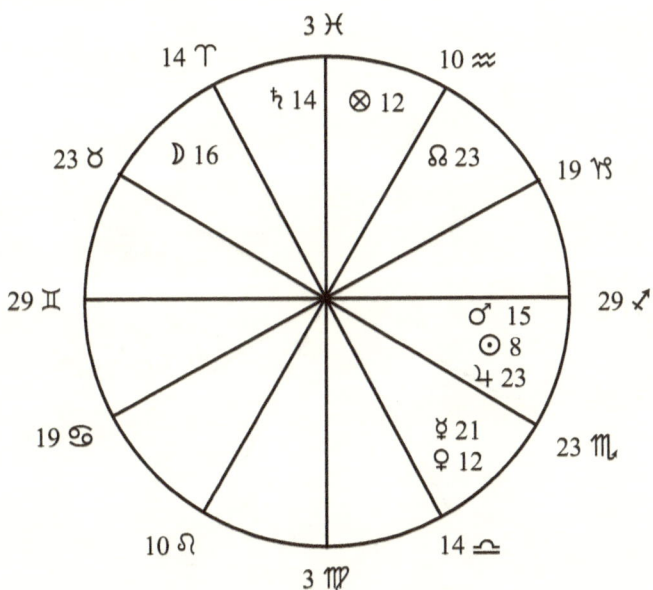

Chart 9.

I looked at the fortune of this Native from the rulers of the Moon's triplicity, the first of which is the Sun, the second is Jupiter, and the third is Saturn. And I found these cadent in the 6th house. It indicates something of evil for him and little good from the testimony of the Part of Fortune, which indicates something evil.

This chart is from the unknown Greek source. It is set for 25 November 464 A.D. at about 6:15 PM LAT (making allowance for the fact that the longitudes from Ptolemy's Tables were about -2° in error). I have redrawn the figure to put the Planets in their proper houses. But calculation shows that Mercury was actually in Sagittarius rather than in Scorpio. The chart is drawn with Alchabitius cusps for 43N that were of course not original.

Abû ᶜAlî's chart is drawn for about an hour earlier with ASC 16°.

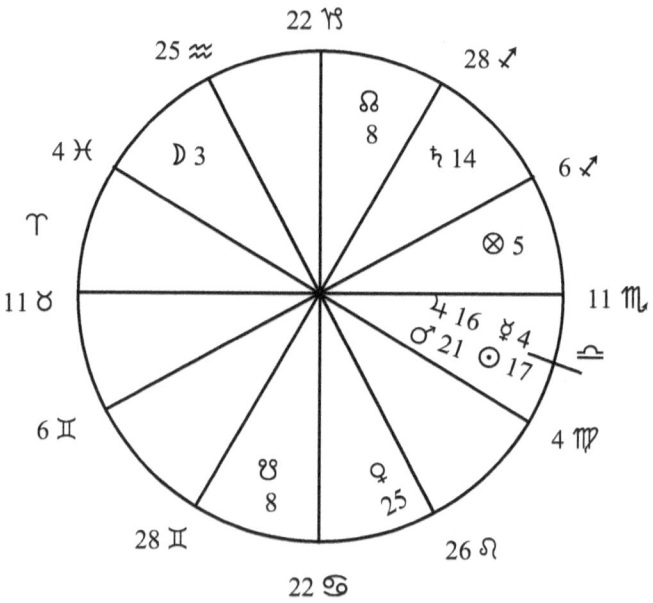

Chart 10.

I looked at the fortune of this [Native] from the rulers of the Moon's triplicity, of which the first is Mars, and it was under the Sun beams in square aspect. It indicates for loss and evil in the first time of his life. And in the second part of his life, it indicates for good, because Venus was the second ruler, and it was in good condition. And it shows that in the second time of his life, he will have good but with much labor. However, Jupiter and Mercury were in the 6th house from the Part of Fortune; and that shows that he will have honor and [good] prospects. So it was.

Mars is under the Sun beams, but not square. And Jupiter and Mercury are in the 6th house from the ASC, not the 6th house from the Part of Fortune.

Mâshâ⟩allâh's chart is set for 8 September 428 at approximately 8:30 P.M.

I have added the degree number of Mars from Abû ⟨Alî's chart, since Mâshâ⟩allâh gives only the sign Virgo. This chart was originally from Rhetorius and is given in Chapter 12 of the MS Parisinus graecus 2506 (ed. in CCAG 8. 1), and the planetary positions were calculated from Ptolemy's Tables. Rhetorius's chart has 25 Taurus 16 rising, which would correspond to about 9:15 P.M. LAT. In both cases the intermediate house cusps were calculated according to the Alchabitius system. This is the earliest chart known to have been originally calculated according to the Alchabitius system!

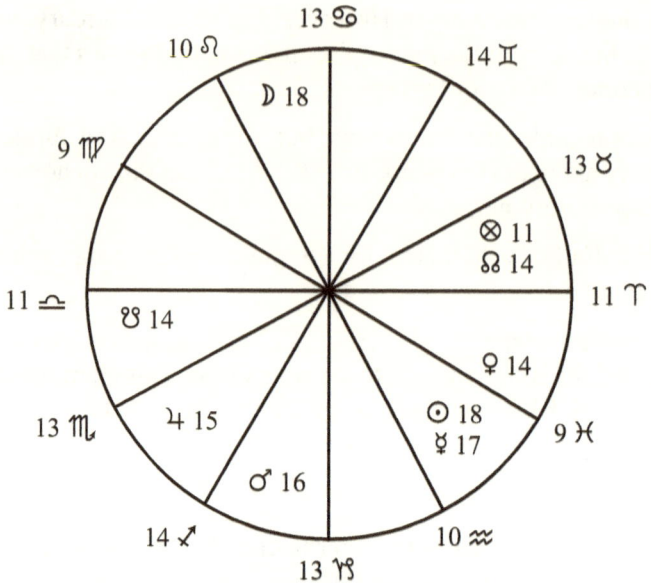

Chart 11.

I looked in the Nativity of this [Native] from the rulers or the Moon's triplicity, the first of which was Mars, and the second was Venus. And I found these to be cadent from the angles. It shows him to have a bad life and loss. Then we looked at the Moon, and it was in the 10th, and the Part of Fortune was in Taurus. It shows that in the last time of his life he will have good.

This chart is from the unknown Greek source. Pingree dates it to 7 February 442 [at about 9:30 P.M. LAT]. but Jupiter was actually then in Sagittarius rather than Scorpio. The intermediate cusps shown in Pingree's figure are Alchabitius cusps for a latitude of 43N and are not original. Abû ᶜAlî puts the ASC at 2 Libra 30.

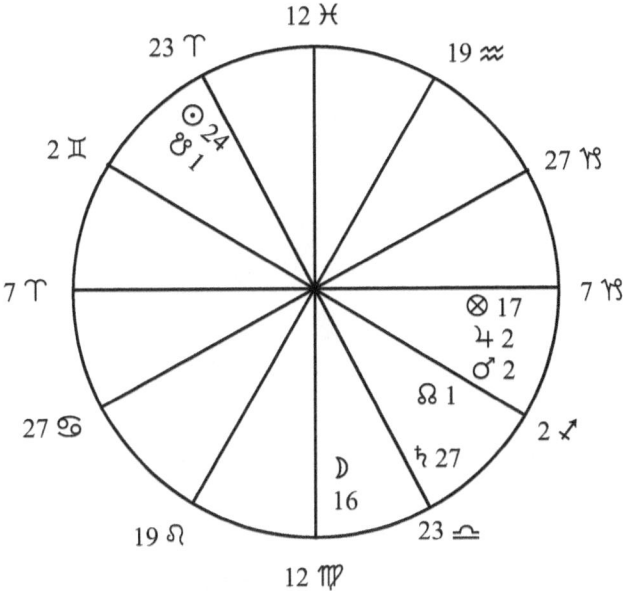

Chart 12.

I looked [at the fortune of this Native] from the rulers of the triplicity of the domicile in which the Sun was, the [ruler] of the first part of it was the Sun, Jupiter was the second ruler, and Saturn was the third. And I looked at the Part of Fortune. It shows him to have good and honor—and more in the middle of his time [of life]. And this appears in the figure.

This chart is probably from the unknown Greek source. It has Alchabitius cusps set for latitude 43N. Mâshâʾallâh's planetary positions are uncertain, and the positions of Mercury and Venus are missing. Pingree suggested a date of 16 April 455, but that puts Saturn in 26 Scorpio, Jupiter at the beginning of Aquarius, and the North Node in Leo. Another possibility is 3 Apr 394 at about 11 A.M. That puts Mars in Taurus and Saturn at 1 Scorpio, but the others (including the North Node) are in the right signs. However, it is probably best to rate this chart as undateable.

INDEX OF PERSONS

BIBLIOGRAPHY

Abu ⁽Ali al-Khayyat
The Judgments of Nativities.
translated by James H. Holden
Tempe, Az.: A.F.A., Inc., 1988. paper 104 pp. diagrs
Tempe, Az.: A.F.A., Inc., 2008. 2nd ed. paper xxviii, 148 pp.
diagrs.

Dorotheus Sidonius
Carmen Astrologicum.
edited and the Arabic version translated
by David Pingree
Leipzig: B. G. Teubner Verlagsgesellschaft, 1976.

Kennedy, E. S. and David Pingree
The Astrological History of Mâshâ⁾allâh.
Cambridge, Mass.: Harvard University Press, 1971.

al-Nadîm
The Fihrist of al-Nadîm.
edited and translated by Bayard Dodge
New York and London: Columbia University Press, 1970. 2 vols.

Ptolemy, Claudius
Tetrabiblos.
edited and translated by F. E. Robbins, Ph.D.
London: William Heinemann Ltd.;
Cambridge, Mass.: Harvard University Press, 1940. xxiv,466 pp.

Sahl ibn Bishr
The Introduction to the Science
of the Judgments of the Stars.
translated by James Herschel Holden
Tempe, Az.: A.F.A., Inc., 2008. paper xxii,214 pp.

MÂSHÂ'ALLÂH

THE BOOK ON THE REVOLUTIONS OF YEARS

Translated from the Twelfth Century Latin Version
of John of Seville

by

JAMES HERSCHEL HOLDEN, M.A.
Fellow of the American Federation of Astrologers

Contents

TRANSLATOR'S PREFACE

Mâshâ⟩allâh was the adopted Muslim name of the Jewish astrologer Mîshâ ibn Athrâ from Basra, Iraq, who converted to Islam and became one of the greatest Arabian[1] astrologers. He was born about 730 A.D. and lived until about 815. He was one of the astrological consultants employed by the Caliph al-Manṣûr (679-777) to make an election for the founding of the new city of Baghdad in 762.[2] Al-Nadîm[3] says this about Mâshâ⟩allâh: "He was a man of distinction and during his period the leading person for the science of judgments of the stars."

He was probably acquainted with the Greek astrologer Theophilus (d. 777), who seems to have been the first prominent Arabian astrologer. Theophilus wrote several books on astrology that survive in Greek versions, but their Arabic versions were unknown to the Twelfth Century Translators, who turned much Arabian astrology into Latin and sparked the recovery of astrology in Western Europe.

Mâshâ⟩allâh thus became the earliest Arabian astrologer whose works were known in the West. He wrote on a variety of subjects and was considered by both later Arabian astrologers and European astrologers to be a prime authority. His *Book on the Revolu-*

---

[1]By *Arabian*, I mean all those, of whatever ethnic group, who wrote in the Arabic language.
[2]See my paper "The Foundation Chart of Baghdad" in *Today's Astrologer* Vol. 65, No. 3 (March 2, 2003): 9-10 & 29.
[3]From the priceless catalogue of Arabic literature as it existed at the end of the 10th century, *The Fihrist of al-Nadîm* edited and translated by Bayard Dodge (New York and London: Columbia University Press, 1970. 2 vols.), II, p. 650.

tion of Years or what is now called *Aries Ingresses* is the earliest Arabian treatise on that subject currently available. It is a comprehensive work.

The first edition of this book was published in 1493 by Bonetus Locatellus at Venice in an omnibus edition of astrological works. I have used a xerox copy of the Latin text included in that edition.

James H. Holden
October 2008

THE REVOLUTION OF THE
YEARS OF THE WORLD

**May God defend You, and may He bless your Life that I am
disclosing to You. May God raise you up high.**

Chapter 1. *The Revolution of the Years of the World.*

The Revolution of the Years of the World, whose knowledge
and arrangement is so that you may know when the Sun enters the
first minute of the sign Aries. And when you have known this, establish the ASC and the four angles and their places by degree and
minutes; and establish the places of the Planets by their own degrees, and their situation according to the order of the circle,
namely their direction; and their retrogradation and slowness and
the transits of some to the others; and their elevation and magnitude and latitude and the projection of their rays. And know that a
retrograde Planet has no strength over good until it is directed.

After that, look at the ASC and the ruler of the exaltation of the
ASC; if it is the exaltation of a Planet and the ruler of the terms and
the ruler of the Triplicity; and the place of the ruler of the hour
from the ASC; and how they are all posited—namely, their places
in turn. And how are those in a place of enmity to the ASC, or that
are in a place of friendship, because if the ruler of the ASC is inimical to the ASC, it signifies detriment in that clime according to the
quantity of enmity; for if it is in the 6th [house]; it will be illness;
and if it is in the 8th, death; and if it is in the 12th, there will be enmity according to the substance of the ruler of the sign in which the

ruler of the ASC is; similarly, if it is the ruler of the terms, and the ruler of the exaltation, and the ruler of the Triplicity; but it will be less than what I have said about the ruler of the ASC.

After that, look at the places of the Lights with respect to the ASC and with respect to the ruler of the ASC. But if the Revolution is by day, and the Sun aspected the ASC or its ruler, and the Sun is free from the malefics, it signifies strength and attainment or victory for the citizens of that same clime; and better still if the Sun gave[1] its disposition to the ruler of the ASC, and if it was received in the place where it was.

But if it was just as we have said, the rich and powerful men of that same clime will be humiliated and subjected by the ruler of that clime; and prosperity will be given to them and peace and health, with good conditions, by the will of God. If the Revolution is by night, in the case of the Moon, it will be similar to what we have said about the Sun. And when the rulers of the Lights or one of them is aspecting it from a strong place, and they are receiving it, there will not be any detriment in men nor any unrest, but they will be untroubled and seeking justice, and making judgments according to it. But if it is the other way around, say the contrary, i.e. turn the good things that we have mentioned into evil things.

And after that, look at the mutual reception of the planets and their enmity in parts; and predict according to what you see for the lands and regions in which it is. And know that the signs signify a [particular] part of the World according to their own natures, not [just] from their own locations, because if a part harmonizes with the nature of a sign, it will be stronger for it.

Aries and its Triplicity of the eastern signs, if they harmonize with the ASC, will be stronger in their signification. Taurus and its Triplicity of the signs of the south, when they harmonize with the signs in the MC, will be stronger for their signification. Gemini

---

[1] Reading *donaverit* 'it gave' instead of *pulsaverit* 'it struck'. This was a common mistranslation of the Arabic verb *dafaʿa*, which can mean 'strike', but also 'hand over' or 'give', and it is the latter meaning that Mâshâʾallâh had in mind. I will make the same correction elsewhere in this translation.

and its Triplicity of the signs of the west, when they harmonize with the signs of the angle of the west, will be stronger for their signification.. Cancer and its Triplicity and the signs of the north, when they harmonize with the IC,[1] will be stronger for their signification. For we say this, when there is in that which we have said a Planet in those places.

And know that there are two divisions of the Earth—rising and in the south is one, because they harmonize with heat—and setting and in the north harmonize with cold. After that, the Earth is divided into climes by the seven divisions of the seven Planets according to the order of the circles; therefore, from the circle the climes are known according to the order of the circles as rulers of the hours. For, the first clime is the clime of Saturn; the second that of Jupiter; the third that of Mars; the fourth that of the Sun; the fifth that of Venus; the sixth that of Mercury; the seventh that of the Moon; but the climes are according to the nature of the circle. Finally, for each one of the lands and cities, something is known.

Similarly too, with the terms, because perhaps there will be a city of some sign, and the terms of some Planet in that same sign will rule it; e.g. as al-ʿIrâq, that is said to be of Cancer, and its Planet is Jupiter; and therefore its Planet is Jupiter, because the place of al-ʿIrâq is from 19 to 27 Cancer, which is the terms of Jupiter; and the position of the benefics in that place signifies good fortune for the citizens of al-ʿIrâq proper. You may know this similarly from the position of the benefics and the malefics in the rest of the terms; and I have already explained that to you. Know therefore that it is just as I have said to you, because when you have done this, you will not be unaware of which sign a city is [signified by] or of which terms.

After that, look to see whether the ascending sign is fixed or mobile or common; and look similarly at the Ruler of the Year, because when the ASC of the year is a mobile sign, the Revolutions

---

[1]The text has 'angle of the earth', which is the common name for the *Imum Caeli* or IC. I will translate it as IC here and hereafter.

of the quarters of the year will be necessary, and all the more if the Ruler of the Year is in a mobile sign. And if the ASC is a common sign, two necessary Revolutions will arise, i.e. the one in the Head of Aries and the one in the Head of Libra; and all the more if the Ruler of the Year is in a common sign. Therefore, make [a chart] at the beginning of the year [and another when the Sun enters] the first minute of the sign Libra. And for mobile [signs], make [charts for] all the quarters of the year.

But when the ASC is a fixed sign, it will be a Revolution of the Year prevailing over all the quarters of the year; and it will be stronger if its ruler is in a fixed sign. But when the Ruler of the Year is a mobile sign, there will be that abundance or scarcity that it signified in the first quarter of the year; nevertheless, unless it is in the second and third and fourth [quarter], the distinction will then be in accordance with that which each of the quarters signified of abundance or scarcity.

Chapter 2. *The Knowledge of the Ruler of the Year.*

When therefore you want to know the Ruler of the Year, look in the hour of the Revolution at the Planet that is stronger than the rest in its own place and with more testimony, and put it as Ruler of the Year in the clime in which you are.

After that, give to the seven climes of the clime in which you are according to that which I have previously said to you of the seven Planets; and I shall explain to you the parts of the planets and their testimony, so that you may know the Ruler of the Year. Know that the stronger Planet is the one that is in the ASC, not remote, nor cadent; or it is the one in the MC. But in the *nadir*[1] and in the IC, it will be below that which I have said to you as its strength by the fourth part; and the 11th sign is below the *nadir* and the IC; and the 9th is below the 11th; and the 5th is below the 9th; and the 3rd is below the 5th.

---

[1]Here Mâshâ'allâh uses the word *nadir* in the sense of *opposite* (namely, *opposite* the MC, which is the IC).

And when the ruler of the ASC is in the ASC, not cadent, nor remote from the angle of the ASC, it will not be [necessary] with it to look at another planet. Similarly, when the ruler of the exaltation is in the degrees of its own exaltation, instead of when the Ruler of the Triplicity is in the ASC or in the MC, it will have a third part of the strength of the ruler of the ASC; also, the ruler of the terms will have a fifth part; and this is according to the quantity of their strength in the signs; and the ruler of the hour has a seventh part. And know that this is when it is in the ASC or in the MC; but if it is in the DSC or in the IC, it will diminish its strength. Similarly, when it is in the 11th, 9th, and 5th, their strength is diminished.

And know that when the Lights are in any of the angles, they will be rulers of the year unless the one that is in an angle is impeded. But if so, it will signify the impediment and debility of that same clime, and the more so if it is the Sun in an angle by day, and the Moon in an angle by night. And similarly, a nocturnal [Planet] flourishes by night; and a diurnal [Planet] flourishes by day. Therefore, when you have been occupied with the Revolutions of Years, begin by [assessing] the strength [of the rulers] according to what I have said to you.

Chapter 3. *When the Ruler of the Year commits its Disposition to another [Planet].*

And when the Ruler of the Year has become known to you, see if it strongly commits its own disposition to another [Planet]; that is, when it is in the domicile of a Planet, and that Planet is in the best place from the ASC, the Ruler of the Year is also joined to it. Because if it is [situated] thus, the ruler of its domicile is made the Ruler of the Year because it receives it from its domicile, and that is better if the Lights aspect it or the rulers of their domiciles; but if it does not commit its own disposition to the ruler of its domicile; look to see whether there is its strength in its own place over the disposition. And its strength is just as I have indicated to you in the first chapter.

When there are planets joined to the Ruler of the Year, and when they commit their own disposition to it, joy will come to that same clime from everywhere over their quantity. And in this case, it will not be necessary for you to look at the other, because it is the Ruler when the Lights commit their disposition to the ruler of the ASC, or the Ruler of the Year without doubt; moreover, you will look for the rustics and their condition from the Ruler of the Year and its place, and from the aspect of the Planets to it.

Chapter 4. *The Significator of the King and his Subjects.*

And you will look for the King of the clime from the ruler of the MC and the Sun, namely from the conjunction and separation of the Planets from them. And from the Sun and the ruler of the MC, you will select the stronger one according to their [individual] strengths, and you will put the selected one as the Significator of the King.

And when you have known the Significator of the King, there will not be unknown to you his condition of good and evil along with that of his rustics; and whatever will come to him in that same year of distribution, distinction, and abundance or scarcity, by the will of God—about every thing, namely concerning his own empire, his own rustics, and his own substance, also concerning his children, and his women, and concerning his health and his illness, his travel, and his strength and weakness, and concerning his demise.

And know that this chapter—that is the chapter about the King—is easier than the chapter on the Ruler of the Year and the condition of his rustics, because you will look at the King as an individual, but you will look at the rustics in general. And when you have known the Ruler of the Year and the Significator of the King of that same region, look at the one that aspects it, and what is its strength in aspecting it, and whether it is in its own light—that is when it will have gone out from under the Sun beams and is joined to no [Planet], nor is in the light of another [Planet]—and whether it is necessary to look at the places of those which will perhaps be the strong Ruler of the Year, [or] whether it is not required.

And I shall explain to you how it will be when the Ruler of the Year is cadent from the ASC and is not aspecting the ASC from the 8th or the 6th or the 2nd or the 12th. Then it will be needed, and therefore a debility will happen for him, because it has fallen into a remote place. And therefore that Planet will be needed to which it is joined—the one that returns its own light to the MC and strengthens it—because a Planet when it has more testimony and is Ruler of the Year, and is in the 8th, then the Planet is [also] needed that aspects it from the MC.

And every Planet that does not aspect the ASC, aspects the MC by trine or sextile aspect, unless it is debilitated in the 3rd and does not aspect. And if the planet that is in the MC is strong and is the ruler of the domicile of the Ruler of the Year, to which testimonies are drawn; and the Ruler of the Year itself is joined to it, it will receive the disposition of the year and its significator; and it will be the Ruler of the Year; and I have already explained this matter to you in the beginning of this book, and how it will be strengthened in its own place by the ruler of its own domicile or by another [Planet].

After that, look at the one that aspects the Ruler of the Year; and pronounce what it will signify in accordance with the quality of the place with respect to good or evil: if it is strong, [it will act] strongly, and if it is weak, weakly.

Chapter 5. *The Significations of Aspects and of the Ruler of the Year and of the rest of the Significators.*

Know that the opposition aspect signifies enmity and contention; and the square is similar; but the trine and the sextile aspect signify friendship. When the malefics aspect the significator of the year or the Significator of the King by opposition, there will be an impediment [for him] from enemies; and if they aspect it by square aspect, it will be from some persons who are thought to be peaceful, whose enmity was previously unknown; and if it is from a trine or sextile aspect, it will be from friends.

After that, look to see whether that impediment enters upon the King or upon the rustics. But if it entered upon the King, look to see whether the rustics will help him or not; but if [instead] it entered upon the rustics, see whether or not the King will help them. After that, look at the same house where the malefic is. If the Significator of the King or the Ruler of the Years has in it any testimony, there will be enmity from its clime according to the quantity of its own testimony.

Look also to see if the Ruler of the Year rules strongly, and it signifies that the King's order will not rule, because if it is so, there will be an enemy from the same clime, but the King is weakened, and another person is introduced into his place. But if the Significator of the King rules, and the Ruler of the Year does not rule, there will not be an enemy from his clime nor from his Kingdom, but the King will bring them under his own domination, and he will subjugate them.

But when you have made this choice, look at the place of the malefic [namely] from which part [of the World] he is, because that very direction from that same part will be from the city or the clime, or from the clime of that same sign. Also, the age of the duke and the principal leader from the bad place may be known from the evil place from the Sun; if it is oriental, he will be a youth; and if it is occidental, he will be an old man.

And pronounce about this what is between them according to what is the place of the Planet: from the connection with the Sun up to its combustion which is evil; also, when it is in the MC and impedites the Ruler of the Year, it will bring this [evil] upon all men; and if it is in the east, that same evil will be from the part of the east; and if it is in the west, it will be from the part of the west; and similarly in the case of the north and south.

And know that nothing is worse for the citizens of the land and the cities which are of the same sign in which the malefic is than that it is retrograde in the Revolution of the Year, and the more so if the malefic is in an angle.

After that, look at the malefic that aspects the Ruler of the Year or the Significator of the King, because if it aspects from the ASC, it signifies that the impediment itself will be in the body; and if it is in the 2nd, on the part of money; and if it is in the 3rd, it will be on the part of brothers; and if it is in the 4th, it will be on the part of parents and inheritance; and if it is in the 5th, on the part of children; and if it is in the 6th, on the part of illnesses; and if it is in the 7th, from war and contention; and if it is in the 8th, on the part of death.

And if there is a malefic in a common sign, it will be feared for the King if his significator aspects it just as I have already said to you. And if the Ruler of the Year is not [also] the significator, it will be feared for the rustics as I have said, because there will be mortality among them. And if it is in the 9th, [it will be] on the part of travel; and if it is in the 10th, on the part of the King and his rule; and if it is in the 11th, on the part of friends; and if it is in the 12th, on the part of enemies. And say similarly of the good that was signified by the will of God. Also, say similarly in the case of a Revolution of the Years of a native, just as I have said to you in the case of a Revolution of the Years of the World.

After that, look at the Ruler of the Year to see in whose domicile it is received, or in what kind of terms or in what kind of exaltation or Triplicity [it is in]. Then look at what kind of place it is in from those that I have mentioned, because when they aspect it and receive it, it will be stronger. After that, look at the sign in which the significator of the year of that clime or of that city is, because the ruler of that clime will be stronger and more effective than the [rulers of the rest of the climes. Finally, put the Planet for each clime, lest it be unknown to you, by the will of God, what will happen to the King of that same clime. And know that stronger than the Ruler of the] King will be the one that is the Ruler of the Year for the clime or the city.

Then look at what follows in succession. And everyone who is born under that same sign on Earth or under the sign of the Ruler of the Year will be useful for good, and there will be security in it unless it is impeded. And when you have done this, look to see who is friendly or unfriendly from the places of the Planets and their aspects, namely from the opposition, and the square, trine and sextile aspect, and from the domiciles from which they are aspecting.

And know that a Planet that is under the Sun beams is similar to one suffering. For when it enters under the beams, its strength recedes, and when it goes out from under the beams, it signifies increase and perfection. And know that it is not the swifter Moon and Mercury of the seven Planets that enjoys good fortune or misfortune; and this is on account of the multitude of their diversity and combustion, because when a Planet's combustion is at its maximum, it signifies evil. And especially every planet that is under the Sun beams, when it is one of those that is the Ruler of the Year and the Significator of the King, and another of the malefics aspects it, then the condition of the year and the King will be worse in this way than it can be [otherwise].

And the Sun, when there is a diurnal Planet under its beams in a Revolution by day, and a nocturnal Planet in a Revolution by night, signifies the King because it then receives the strength of the Planets. And if the ruler of the domicile of the ASC is under the Sun beams, the Sun will be more dignified in the year. And best of all, look at the places of the Lights [and] the aspects of the rulers of their domiciles to each other, and their mutual aspects.

Look also to see whether there is [one that is] strong, because the Planet will be the stronger by aspect, when it aspects from its own domicile or exaltation or from its own Triplicity or terms or from [some other] place of strength, or when it is the ruler of the Part of Fortune. And [look] when it is with that which I have said, and [is also] oriental or direct; for then it will be stronger than it can be [otherwise].

Look too at the Part of Fortune and its ruler and their places in the signs, because these strengthen the Ruler of the Year and the Significator of the King; but if they are impeded, look at them and their places in the signs, because the Part of Fortune is the strength of the Lights. But if they were joined together in a fortunate place, it signifies good and advantage; and if they were impeded under the Sun beams, they signify detriment and loss according to the substance of the signs in which they are located.

After that, look at the Ruler of the Year to [see to] which [Planet] it is joined, because partly from that there will be confidence or fear. Look also to see if perhaps the Ruler of the Year is the Significator of the King. And I shall explain to you how this can be—namely when the Ruler of the Year is having testimony in the MC, or when it is the ruler of the exaltation of the MC, or when the ruler of the MC commits its disposition and its own strength, or when the ruler of the MC is in its own domicile aspecting it. For when it is thus, the Ruler of the Year will be the Significator of the King.

And when you have known this in a Revolution of Years, know the Significator of the King from the Ruler of the Year. And know his condition from the condition of the rustics. But if the Sun is the Ruler of the Year, look just as I have told you in the first chapter. Look also at the ruler of the MC [to see] if it is under the Sun beams entering into combustion—that signifies the death of the King! And if it has already gone out of combustion and does not [yet] appear, the Sun will be more worthy than it of being the Significator of the King.

After that, look at the one to which the Significator of the King is joined, because when it is connected to the Ruler of the Year, he entrusts his own things to the rustics. And if it is separated from the Ruler of the Year and is joined to a malefic or to a Planet that is unfriendly to the ASC, he will suspect them and he will put an impediment onto them.

And if the Significator of the King is joined to any Planet in the 8th or the 6th by opposition or square aspect, the death of the King will be feared for in that same year. Similarly, if it is also joined to their rulers outside of the places that I have mentioned to you; and it will be even stronger if they are joined to malefics, and illness will have to be feared for him if it is joined to a Planet in the 3rd or the 6th, just as I have said in the first chapter, or to their rulers.

Similarly, you will look at every one of his conditions in this manner, and at what I have said if the ruler of the MC commits its own disposition to the Ruler of the Year. But if the ruler of the MC does not commit its disposition, it will be more dignified than that which I have said. Look also at the 12th house for the region for disadvantage and abundance and for fear and sorrow. And look, therefore, at all the regions of the climes and the parts.

After that, look to see which is the ruler of the domicile of the Ruler of the Year, because if it aspects and receives it, joy and security will find them; and if it does not aspect it, fear and disadvantage will find them. But if the Ruler of the Year commits its disposition to the Significator of the King, it will let loose disadvantage upon them on account of the acquisition of wealth, when its committing is by square aspect or by opposition; but if its disposition is by trine or sextile aspect, it will signify the return of wealth without the inroad of disadvantage to the rustics.

And if it commits its own disposition without an aspect, this will occur without the knowledge of the King; and if it aspects the ruler of its domicile, the King will remove wealth in that same year; and if it does not aspect, he will remove wealth without his own ill will. After that, look at the condition of the King to see if the Significator of the King is the ruler of the MC and look to see if the Ruler of the Year is from the 2nd. And the condition of the soldiers with regard to the King is [known] from the ruler of the sign in which it is, and from the ruler of the terms or the face; and it will be helped in this by the Part of Fortune and its rulers, which if the Significator of the King aspects it or is with it, it signifies good fortune for the King.

Similarly, look at [the condition of] the rustics from the Ruler of the Year. And know the condition of the King from his own significator, and [the condition] of the powerful persons and the nobles from the Ruler of the Year, because when you have done this, their condition will not be unknown to you, and what will be found for them of good and evil in that year, and in what way or by what kind of cause, if God wills it.

After that, look at the Ruler of the Year and the Significator of the King. If they are retrograde, they signify loss and debility for the King and for the citizens of his Kingdom. But if they are both retrograde, or one of them is, look to see in whose terms it is retrograde—namely, whether it is in the terms of a benefic or a malefic—and similarly take into account in your work the ruler of the domicile, because if there is a retrograde Planet in the domicile of a benefic, it will be better than [if it is] in the domicile of a malefic or in the terms of a malefic, because the retrogradation of the Significator of the King signifies the weakness of the King; and the retrogradation of the Ruler of the Year signifies the weakness of his rulership.

After that, look for war in the part [of the World] in which Mars was if it was direct; and it will be with determined men who do not want to flee; and if it is retrograde, it will be with armed robbers, who do not remain quiet in one place, and who do not enter into war.

But Saturn signifies difficulty for the citizens of the region in which it is according to the substance of the sign in which it is and its place in the houses by succession, such as the ASC and the House of Substance, until it comes to the 12th. And when it is retrograde, it will be just as I have said to you about Mars. And it will be more serious [depending upon its] connection; and if it is connected to the Ruler of the Year, it will be more serious for the King in the lands and the clime in which it is.

After that, look at attainment and victory from the stronger one of the Planets, because that one signifies the multitude of the soldiers and their strength, just as you look at the testimony of the Planets and their strength in their own places. After that, look at the swiftness of victory and its slowness from Jupiter and Saturn and the testimonies of their conjunction and the condition of their profection in the radix according to their course.

And in the major years of the cycle, in which a middling conjunction is made that changes from one Triplicity into another, by their profection in the radix, there is made a change of sects and Kingdoms. For there is signified that which I have told you about their conjunction in three ways; and I shall explain this to you in the following chapter.

And when you have done all this just as you do in the Revolution of Years of a Nativity according to the radix of a nativity, you will get the significations of sects and Kingdoms from the conjunction of Saturn and Jupiter and their mutation from one Triplicity to another.

Look also at the presence of the three Planets that are above the Sun and their places in the fixed, mobile, and common signs, and put it in the hour of the destruction of things. And I shall show [this to] you in the course of Saturn and Mars; and I shall explain all these things to you. Know that when [one of] the malefics—namely Saturn and Mars—are in a sign of the image of men, and another malefic is conjoined to it, and it is direct or retrograde from the conjunction, or in square aspect or opposition, there will be pestilence among men. But if it is retrograde, it will be more active[1] and swifter; and you ought to look to see whether there is an aspect and connection from any one of the angles; and if so, it will be more active and stronger; look then to see in which angle it is.

Moreover, if Saturn, which is slower, is in the 4th or in the MC, and the retrograde Planet that is joined to it is in the 7th, that evil will come from the part of the west, and the thing will be signified and strengthened; and if the slower one is in the west, and the retrograde [Planet] that is joined to it is in the 4th, that [evil] will begin in the region that I have said to you until it comes to the west.

After that, look at the manner of its beginning from the part of the swifter Planet that is joined to the heavier one. And know that the second malefic will come to the places of the slower and

[1]Reading *calidius* 'more active' instead of *callidius* 'more crafty'.

weightier one; and know that [from the] one that is retrograde and conjunct, i.e. the one that is joined, when it is in a common sign, there will be death from war or killing; and in fixed signs it will be immobile according to what the stronger one of the malefics signified in its own places.

If it is Mars, it will be stronger for war or for an illness that is feverish. But if it is Saturn, death will stronger from every kind of illness that is of the likeness of Saturn. And mix with it the strength of Mars; and if what I have said is beyond an angle, it will be middling [in severity] after it abates, if God wills.

Chapter 6. *The Severity of the Revolution of the Years of the World.*

When you want to make a Revolution of the Years of the World in which there is something to be feared, look to see whether in that year there is a conjunction of Saturn and Jupiter, and whether it will be more evil, and if not, will it be more gentle. Similarly, when the Ruler of the Year or the Significator of the King transits a slow and evil Planet in an angle, it will be feared for the significator then, just as I have said to you about destruction and death.

Look also at the malefics; if they are in such a condition as I have said to you above in their nocturnal place or their diurnal place, because Saturn in a diurnal and masculine sign is less of an impediment; and Mars in a feminine sign and a nocturnal place, is less of an impediment. After that, look to see whether they are received in their own places or not, because if they are received, their impediment will be less; and if there is illness in that same year, only a few will die; and if they signify killing, there will be wounds and not killing, except for a small amount; and there will be wailing among men.

And know that the Head of the Dragon harmonizes with the benefics, and the Tail of the Dragon[1] aids the malefics; therefore, look at a conjunction of the Head and Saturn, because it signifies

---

[1]The Head of the Dragon is the Moon's North Node, and the Tail of the Dragon is the Moon's South Node.

according to the substance of the sign in which they are joined, just as it signifies in the case of eclipses of the Lights; for when it is just as I have said to you in Aries and its Triplicity, [the difficulty] will be with wild animals and wolves according to the substance of the sign in which they are conjoined. And if it is in Taurus and its Triplicity, it will be with trees and plants, and there will be few rains and a small harvest. And if they are conjoined in air signs, there will be impediment for men and birds, and the winds will blow. And in water signs, the rains and waters and fish and cold spells will be multiplied; and locusts and the serpents[1] of the Earth will be multiplied.

And look at the square aspect of the malefic and the Tail and their conjunction, because they will strongly signify war and famine and a multitude of fear, and there will be great cold and a multitude of evil. And if Saturn is conjoined with the Tail, it signifies famine and scarcity of good, and the strength of cold, and the destruction of trees, and it will be in the part [of the land] in which it is; and if the Sun makes a Planet combust in it, this will be stronger in that part [of the land] than in the rest of the parts.

And know that the slower Planet signifies war; and a retrograde [Planet] signifies flight, but a direct [Planet] signifies peace, and especially if a benefic aspects it from the MC, and if the ruler of its domicile, or the ruler of its Triplicity, or the ruler of its terms, or the ruler of the exaltation aspects the Planet, it signifies a multitude of helpers from nearby as well as others, according to that quantity that I have said to you.

Look also at the condition of the ruler of the army from the planets from which the signification is taken, because when the planet is in its own domicile, it will be from the members of the King's household, and it will be known; and if it is in its own exaltation, it will be a noble useful to the Kingdom; and if it is in its own Triplicity, it will be someone below what I have said, but he will be a known person, and he is below them; and if it is not

---

[1]Reading *serpentia* 'serpents' instead of *repentia* 'unexpected things'.

anything from that which I have said, he will not be known nor high-born; and it may perhaps be said of him that he is born from fornication.

And know that the diurnal Planets, the Sun, Saturn, and Jupiter, are also masculine by day. And the nocturnal Planets, the Moon, Mars, and Venus, are also feminine by night. But Mercury is masculine with masculine Planets, and feminine with feminine Planets; and also, nocturnal with nocturnal Planets, and diurnal with diurnal Planets.

Chapter 7. *A Chapter on Fear for the King.*

When in the Revolution of the Year the Significator of the Year enters into combustion, the King of that same region will die; and if it is at the summit of its rays, sorrow and sadness will come upon him. But if a benefic aspects it, he will escape that. And if it is more than what I have said to you, and it has already passed through combustion, anger and contention will come upon him, [but] afterwards he will be freed from it, and his condition will be bettered, unless a malefic aspects it, because then it signifies a prolongation of those things that I have said and their extension; and it must be feared for him according to the nature of the sign—either it will be an illness or death.

Therefore, look at the hour of this signification from the time of the conjunction of the significator and the malefic. And similarly, when a malefic aspects the Significator of the King from an opposition or square aspect or from conjunction, it will be feared for him when it is with that which I have said in an angle.

And the time of that will be the combustion of the significator, and in the advent of that same malefic at the place of the significator, or at the MC, or at the ASC, unless it is aided by a benefic in aspect. And that same malefic is a helper in its nature, and whichever one is malefic, that one will be the Significator of the King, because difficulty will come upon men from the part of the King, and it will be stronger if it is in an angle—for then it signifies that it will not be worn down by their difficulty. And if it is in the MC with that which I have said to you, there will be difficulty from some foreigners; and this will be in the place of the malefic if it is in the East, and similarly if it is in the West; and if it is in the MC, it will be universal for all men, and especially in the part of *benethnas*,[1] i.e. Ursa Major, by which is signified the North, as if it would say in the part of the North; and if it is in the part of the IC, it will be in the East and Hot Land,[2] i.e. [the land] of the Blacks, and similarly benefics, unless they are retrograde and in a bad place, i.e. in their own falls, or in the oppositions to their own domiciles,[3] because these are their inimical places, because they are then debilitated.

[It is necessary] therefore to look at the parts in which they are; and look at the Planet by which the King and his condition are signified; and pronounce on the condition of the Planets and their perfection on each day for difficulty and want, or for abundance of good or evil. After that, look at the reception of the Lights and its bestowing, because that signifies what will happen to the rustics.

Chapter 8. *A Question about War and Which of Two will Win.*

And if you are asked about a war—whether it will take place—and which one of them will get the victory? Look for the one for whom you want to look, at what his condition is in that same year, and in what way the Significator of the King and the Ruler of the Year aspects it; Which, if it is in a strong place and the Significator of the King does not aspect it, and the Ruler of the Year does aspect it over the Ruler of the Question, the King will be severe, and the King will not aid him, but there will be helpers from the King's staff. and if the Significator of the King aspects it, pronounce the King's anxiety for him according to the aspect of strength or debility; but if they are inimical in nature, say that he

---

[1] From the Arabic *banât na'sh al-kubrâ* 'daughters of the Great Bear' (the Arabic name for Ursa Major), a northern constellation.

[2] The Latin has *accenden*, perhaps from *accendo* 'to set on fire'. Here probably it means 'in the South'.

[3] That is, in their *detriments*.

will be injured by him; and if they are peaceful, judge according to what you see.

And therefore they indicate that to you so that you may marvel; and you know how you are looking at these matters, because there is nothing hidden from you from that method of its description. And know reasonably of its flaws, just as I have already said to you in the chapter on Revolutions to what extent you will not dismiss destruction nor attainment when you look at it; and you may see with what the aid of the planets will be for him according to their[1] substance by the length or brevity of their rulership.

Chapter 9. *A Question about the Impediment of Mortality and in how many Parts they are dying.*

And know that a Planet that is under the Sun beams will impedite the citizens of that same clime; and it will destroy their condition and make them to be subjugated, and all the more so if a malefic is in an angle of the Revolution or if it aspects it, because if it is under the Sun beams in the way that I have said to you, and it is at the end of the sign in which it is posited, and a malefic before it aspects it, and another malefic after it, this clime will suffer according to the quantity of the aspect of the malefic.

For, if it is conjoined in one sign, all of them will perish; and if it is in opposition, half of them; but if it is by square aspect, a fourth part of them. Moreover, if Saturn precedes and Mars is after it, they will be captured, and they will not be killed by them, except for a few. But if Mars precedes and Saturn is after it, the whole lot of them will be killed.

After that, look at the malefic that aspects the Significator of the King; if it aspects it from the sign in which the testimony of the King is, it will be an enemy from his land according to the quantity of its testimony. And if it aspects from the domicile of the Significator of the King, it will be from his own staff. And if it aspects him from its own exaltation, it will be from those nobles who

---

[1]Reading *eorum* 'their' instead of *deorum* 'of the gods'.

are his counselors and [persons] of his order; but [if its aspects from] a Triplicity and terms, it signifies some of his own citizens.

And know that the trine and sextile aspect signifies those who are close; and the opposition signifies enemies; and the first square aspect signifies the house of his parents; but the second square signifies high-born persons and well-born councilors from among those who are close to the Kingdom. In the case of the conjunction, look at the sign about which we have spoken; for if there is testimony for it in it, it will be from those who are close—from, those who were raised with him. And if there is no testimony for it, it will be one of their offspring. Best of all, look at these chapters.

After that, look at the places of the Lights, their order, and their separation, and the conjunctions to which they are joined; and in what manner they are separated, because the connection by the sextile or trine aspect is weak; but the opposition and conjunction is strong.

Best of all, look at this chapter, because it signifies the quantity of their strength. And I shall disclose to you all the work of the seven planets and their signification. The Sun signifies the King. The Moon signifies all of the common people. Jupiter signifies nobles; Mars signifies warriors. Saturn signifies those of religious faith. Venus signifies women. Mercury signifies businessmen and boys.

Look therefore when there are any of these significators, whether it has a part in that same year, because if it does have a part in that same year, there will come into it that which I have said to you about difficulty and detriment. And the part of it is as it is in the ASC or in the MC by its own degree and sign, except Venus and the Moon, because one of them, when it is in its own domiciles in the DSC or in the IC, very strongly signifies impediment, because these two are forefathers; and Mars is similar, but it is below them. Jupiter, moreover, and Saturn, and even more so the Sun, will be their condition, when the ASC and the MC are in their domiciles.

Every masculine Planet in the East will be stronger, and similarly their domiciles; and similarly, the feminine Planets are stronger in the West; and it will be all the more so for them in the meridian, and similarly their domiciles.

Chapter 10. *The Division of the World and the Climes by the Substance of the Planets and Signs.*

Know that the World is divided into three divisions according to the substances of the three planets that are above the Sun, namely according to their substances and their complexions. Therefore, the higher part of the World is Saturn's; and the middle part is Jupiter's, and it is the temperate part, similar in substance to Jupiter; but the lower part is that of Mars, which is the hot part, and it is according to the substance of Mars.

And the Moon participates with Saturn in its own part, because her sign is opposed to his own sign; therefore, for the quality of the year of the citizens of that part [of the World], there is a scarcity of wisdom and certitude and a cutting off of piety and forgetfulness. Also, their colors are red and white; and similarly, there is whiteness and forgetfulness in them. For their complexion is from the darkness of the land and the air.

And Mercury participates with Jupiter, because his domicile is opposed to Jupiter's. Also, the quality of the mind of the citizens of that part is wisdom and certitude and religion and truth, and the conjunction of piety and acuity of intellect. And their colors are of various complexions mixed, namely from whiteness and blackness and redness, just as their domiciles are mixed from the coldness of the Earth and the heat of the air. Of these divisions, it is therefore more worthy and propitious than the rest of the divisions. And their land is better than the rest of the lands, being the land of the prophets and wise men. And Venus participates with Mars, because her domicile is opposed to his domicile, just as we have said; also, the quality of mind of the citizens of that same part is one of disgrace and venereal desire and drinking and play, according to the places of those same Planets. And their colors are burnt from the heat of the Earth and the air. And the Sun participates with Jupiter and Mercury in their parts.

The climes are also divided according to these modes in their secular quality and the colors of the bodies according to the order of the circles in their latitude. After that, the twelve signs are also divided, which are circles or parts of the gate; and in these, there are 360 paths divided by the degrees of the Sun; and there are 21,600 gates or medium smaller parts[1]; but they are not needful, except in the case of the Revolution of the World and in the Revolution of the Year; in the chapters of the Sun, it must be taken into account in the equation of the Sun, so that you will not be lacking the [exact] degree of the ASC and the [time] of the quarters [of the year].

Also, the East and its wind is hot and dry, the West and its wind is cold and humid. The South and its wind is hot and humid. The North and its wind is cold and dry. And similarly, Aries and its Triplicity is hot and dry. Taurus and its Triplicity is cold and dry. Gemini and its Triplicity is hot and humid. Cancer and its Triplicity is cold and humid. They have also stated that in the seven climes, that is the [whole] World, there are cities and castles and villages according to the number of the 12 signs of Heaven, just as there are 12 signs that are those of the great cities, of which there are in each one of the climes, 2 of Saturn, 2 of Jupiter, 2 of Mars, 1 of the Sun, 2 of Venus, 2 of Mercury, and 1 of the Moon.

And I shall make plain to you how many cities and castles and villages they have said there are in the 7 climes. For in the 1st clime, they have said there are 3100. And in the 2nd clime, 1713; in the 3rd clime, 1077; in the 4th clime, 2944; in the 5th clime, 3006; in the 6th clime, 3408; and in the 7th clime, 3300.[2]

---

[1]These are of course the minutes of the 360 degrees.
[2]The total number of the inhabited places in the World is 18,548 according to these figures.

Chapter 11. *The Signification of the Ruler of the Year and of each Planet when it is the Ruler of the Year.*

Look therefore at the Revolution. If the Sun commits its disposition to the Moon, i.e. if the Revolution is by night, look at the Moon and its place from the ASC; to see if it is suitable to be the ruler of the disposition; look at the ruler of its domicile and the aspect of the planets to it; and say according to what you see from the aspect of the malefics and the benefics and their connection; and look at its place and Saturn's, what sort it is, namely whether it is joining to it or being separated from it.

Look at the increase or diminution of its light. Look also to see whether an eclipse may happen to it in that same year or not. After that, look at the eclipse of the Moon and its place and the eclipse of the Sun and its place, and the aspect of the planets to it.

And know that when the Ruler of the Year in that same year is impeded, it will exert its detriment on the rustics and it will weigh down upon their condition according to the substance of that same sign in that same land which is of that same sign, as for example Libra when it is the ASC of the year, and Venus is cadent or retrograde or under the Sun beams, the land of Libra will be destroyed, and illness will occur in it and sorrows.

After that, look at every sign according to the condition of its ruler and its place from it, and their agreement and detriment; it will act according to the aspect of the Planets to it. And speak about this according to what you see; and when you explain about these things, look at the 2nd sign and its ruler, then at the 3rd sign and its ruler, in the manner in which I have said, until you come to the 12th sign; and you should look more closely at the signs on the angles, because there is more strength in them than in the rest of the signs.

And know that when Mars in the hour of the Revolution is in the MC, this will signify that the King is putting someone under physical restraint[90]; and if it is in the ASC or in the DSC angle, he will

---

[90]The Latin has *in patibulo*. The *patibulum* was a forked-shaped yoke placed on the neck of criminals.

cut off the hands[1] of some in his own Kingdom; and in the IC, he will kill them. And when it is Saturn in the ASC. it signifies famine and death and illnesses and violent and harmful winds. And when the ruler of the ASC and the Ruler of the Year is Mercury, and it is free from the malefics, and the benefics aspect it, it will be a good year, and one useful for wise men and merchants and boys, and all the more so if it is received by the ruler of the domicile in which it is posited. And if the reverse is true, say the contrary.

And when it is the Moon in the ASC, and it is the Ruler of the Year and free from the malefics, rains will be multiplied and cold, and rivers will overflow; and [the people] will find good and joy, and all the more so if it is received. And if it is Jupiter in the ASC, it will be a year of drought, and things will go well for men and rich persons, and they will profit; and if it is received, the majority of the common people will find good from the King; and they will admire their own King. And if it is Mars in the ASC, there will be an earthquake in that same land, and the rains will be scanty; and there will be a middling amount of war. And if it is the Sun in the ASC, or if it is the Ruler of the Year, and it is free from the malefics, the rich persons will rejoice, and good will abound, and things will go well. But if it is impeded, it will also be what I have said, but the contrary of it.

And know also that years are oppressive when there are malefics in the upper part of the chart and not in the lower part; and especially if Mars commits its own disposition to Saturn, because it signifies oppressive and prolonged things from the appearance of detriment on Earth, and the debility of the King, and the taking away of faith and religion. And armed robberies and contentions will be multiplied, and especially if there is any one of the malefics in the MC.

And along with this, look at the Moon, because when she commits her disposition to Saturn from the lower part of the chart under the Earth, it signifies trouble and detriment and change in the

---

[1] A not uncommon punishment in Muslim countries.

Kingdom; and if the Moon gives her own light to Saturn and is with him, or in square aspect [to him], or in opposition to him, there will be detriment. And similarly, look at the Sun just as you have looked at the Moon, because if it is received, it signifies the taking away of evil. And know that the benefics signify the loosening of evil and the taking away of it if they are strong in their own place and of good testimony; and if they are direct, they signify good and accommodation.

And know that when a Planet emerges from being under the Sun beams—i.e. from combustion—it will be like a boy who progresses and grows, if then, no malefics aspect it. And similarly, when it enters into being under the Sun beams and combustion, it will be like an old man becoming weaker. Therefore, consider this chapter particularly well.

After that, look at the entrance of each Planet into its own exaltation and close to Saturn, because then it is made stronger; and look at what testimony and strength it has if it is receiving testimony and disposition, because it will then signify greater things; and similarly, Jupiter and the rest of the Planets.

And when the year is revolved, look at the benefics and the malefics; if they are aspecting from a fixed sign, that which they signify of good or evil will be prolonged; and if they are aspecting from a mobile sign, it will be middling; but if they are aspecting from a common sign, it will be intermediate.

After that, look at the matter of an eclipse according to the quantity of substance of the ASC, when you would know what will be in that same year of the eclipse. Look so that you will see the ruler of the sign in which the eclipse will be—what its condition may be, and what sort of place it is in, and its condition from the ruler of the ASC of the eclipse, and what sort of condition it may be in from the Ruler of the Year and the Significator of the King, and in what way the benefics or the malefics aspect it. Because, if it is impeded by an aspect of the malefics, that which they will signify will be aggravated and multiplied, and all the more so if the ruler of the domicile of the eclipse is the Significator of the King.

But if it is the Significator of the King, and there are malefics aspecting it, it must be feared for him when the Sun comes to the MC of the eclipse. And if it is the Ruler of the Year, it must be feared for the rustics when the Sun comes to the ASC of the eclipse according to the quantity of the substance of the ASC. If it is [in a sign that is] an image of men, there will be impediment among men; and if it is [in a sign that has] the substance of animals, [the impediment] will be among animals; and if it is [in a sign that has] the substance of water, [the impediment] will be in waters according to the quantity of the substance of the ASC sign.

And know that for each hour of the hours of an eclipse of the Moon, there will be a distinction for each hour—namely, for one month; and for an eclipse of the Sun, for each hour, a year. After that, look at the malefics; if they are in the ASC or close to the ASC, there will be an impediment in the middle part, which we have said.

INDEX OF PERSONS

BIBLIOGRAPHY

al-Nadîm
The Fihrist of al-Nadîm.
edited and translated by Bayard Dodge
New York and London: Columbia University Press, 1970. 2
vols.

MÂSHÂ'ALLÂH

THE BOOK ON THE SIGNIFICATION OF THE PLANETS IN THE NATIVITY

Translated from the Twelfth Century Latin Version
of John of Seville

by

JAMES HERSCHEL HOLDEN, M.A.
Fellow of the American Federation of Astrologers

Contents

*The Signification of the Planets in their own Terms
or in those of Another Planet*

TRANSLATOR'S PREFACE

Mâshâ'allâh was the adopted Muslim name of the Jewish astrologer Mîshâ ibn Athrâ from Basra, Iraq, who converted to Islam and became one of the greatest Arabian[1] astrologers. He was born about 730 A.D. and lived until about 815. He was one of the astrological consultants employed by the Caliph al-Manṣûr (679-777) to make an election for the founding of the new city of Baghdad in 762.[2] Al-Nadîm[3] says this about Mâshâ'allâh: "He was a man of distinction and during his period the leading person for the science of judgments of the stars."

He was probably acquainted with the Greek astrologer Theophilus (d. 777), who seems to have been the first prominent Arabian astrologer. Theophilus wrote several books on astrology that survive in Greek versions, but the Arabic versions were unknown to the Twelfth Century Translators, who turned much Arabian astrology into Latin and sparked the recovery of astrology in Western Europe. Hence, Theophilus is largely unknown to modern astrologers.

Mâshâ'allâh thus became the earliest Arabian astrologer whose works were known in the West. He wrote on a variety of subjects and was considered by both later Arabian astrologers and Euro-

---

[1]By *Arabian*, I mean all those, of whatever ethnic group, who wrote in the Arabic language.
[2]See my paper "The Foundation Chart of Baghdad" in *Today's Astrologer* Vol. 65, No. 3 (March 2, 2003): 9-10 & 29.
[3]From the priceless catalogue of Arabic literature as it existed at the end of the 10th century, *The Fihrist of al-Nadîm* edited and translated by Bayard Dodge (New York and London: Columbia University Press, 1970. 2 vols.), II, p. 650.

pean astrologers to be a prime authority. His *Book on the Significations of the Planets in the Nativity* is the earliest available Arabian treatise on the Significations of the Planets in the domiciles of the Planets, the Significations of the House Rulers in all twelve Houses, and the Significations of the Planets in the terms of the Planets.

Whether these significations are Mâshâ'allâh's own work or whether they are based on some Greek books that had been translated into Arabic is unknown. Similar but more extensive significations of the Planets were given in Julius Firmicus Maternus's *Mathesis*, Book V, where they were translated from some earlier Greek astrological texts. Unfortunately, while Saturn in the signs is complete, Jupiter in the signs leaves off after Jupiter in Capricorn, and the significations of Mars, the Sun, Venus, Mercury, and the Moon in the signs, and then of Saturn, Jupiter, the Sun, Mars, and Venus in the terms, are missing in the great lacuna in *Mathesis* Book V.

The first edition of the Latin version of Mâshâ'allâh's book on the Significations of the Planets was published in 1493 by Bonetus Locatellus at Venice in an omnibus edition of astrological works. It was edited by Joachim Heller and reprinted by Montanus & Neuber in a nicer format at Nürnberg in 1549. I have used a copy of the Latin text included in that edition.

James H. Holden
Phoenix, Arizona

The Significations of the Planets in their own Signs and in the Signs of other Planets.

Chapter 1. *The Signification of Saturn in his own Sign or in the Sign of Others.*

When Saturn is in his own domicile, his actions will be strong; and the Native will be associated with those who know the sciences. And if it was a nativity by day, he will be stronger; and if it was by night he will be sorrowful.

If Saturn is in a domicile of Jupiter, it signifies that the Native will live long, and he will have much wealth; and he will have honor before princes if he is born by day; but if he is born by night, he will experience poverty and the loss of his paternal inheritance.

If Saturn is in a domicile of Mars, the Native will be exuberant; and he will experience a loss in his paternal inheritance; and he will see the death of his own succession.

If Saturn is in the domicile of the Sun, he will be born with an open face; and he will be a mocker as it were, and a joker, and he will be irascible. And he will have little expectation or stability. And if he is born by day, he will be in good circumstances and with much good fortune; and the actions of his father will be good; and if he is born by night, he will not have any honor, but [instead] he will have lawsuits and toil, and be hindered by his brother.

If Saturn is in a domicile of Venus, his actions with women will be evil; and he will accept old women [as wives]; and he will delight in intercourse with old women, skinny women, and disgraceful women. And he will hear bad words spoken [about him] because of that; and he will see disgrace.

If Saturn is in a domicile of Mercury, his speech will be serious; and he will be of calm judgment; and he will be fond of philosophers and astronomers and the discovery of causes or games. And he will see deeply into things; and he will investigate the sciences; and from that he will suffer loss. His mind or his speech will be made serious; and he will have some evil association, and whatever is said about it, he will quickly believe.

If Saturn is in the domicile of the Moon, he will have some scandal with women and with his associates. And his illness will be from phlegm and in his spleen, and in his lower parts, or his illness will be in the parts below the navel; and it will be similar for his mother. And it will cause a loss in the mother's wealth.

Chapter 2. *The Signification of Jupiter when it is in its own Domicile or in those of the other Planets.*

If Jupiter is in a domicile of Saturn, he will have moderate honor; and he will serve princes and greater men; and he will be a person of many thoughts, and greedy; and he will endure a great loss. And he will toil so that his poverty is apparent; and he will be of bad judgment, careless, and very slack and dull; and he will do his own work privately; and account of that, he will incur loss

If Jupiter is in his own domicile, he will be in [a state of] goodness and good fortune, good actions, honor, and riches. And if it is by day, it will be more profitable, and if a malefic does not aspect it, he will have much honor before princes. And if it is by night, the things said above will be small; and he will make his way in life step by step; and if he is chosen for anything, a religious place will come to him from it.

And if Jupiter is in a domicile of Mars, he will be honored and elevated; and he will be fond of those who know about laws; and he will serve learned men and greater men; and he will be joined in friendship with the king or with a prince. And he will be a drinker of wine.[1] And he will do those things that are mostly praised by all. And his lying or sitting near[2] and his elevation will be with princes. And if the Sun or the Moon is in the angles or in the succedents, he will be like a prince; and his name will be spread abroad in the world.

If Jupiter is in the domicile of the Sun, he will be honorable and wise; and he will have a good reputation with princes and great men. And if it is in an angle and is not impedited, he will be very rich; and he will be great just like a prince, or he will be compared to people like that; and this will be more likely if the nativity of this boy is by day.

If Jupiter is in a domicile of Venus, he will run about[3] much; and if the Native is a male, his association, namely his sitting and standing will be with princes; and he will have honor and dignity; and he will take a wife for some time who will have great honor; and he will see much delight; and he will have wealth from women. And if the native is a woman, she will be a religious person and like a nun, and of good faith, and honest; and from that [characteristic] she will encounter goodness.

If Jupiter is in a domicile of Mercury, it signifies a man who is great in teaching; it signifies he is in charge of great men; and he will have soldiers; and he will be a merchant, or a striker of money[4]; and he will get many things and give many things. And he will be a philosopher and a wise man; and he will be like a prince; and he will acquire much wealth.

If Jupiter is in the domicile of the Moon, he will have goodness and greatness and much wealth; and his sitting and standing will be with princes and great men; and it will be better if Jupiter is in angles or succedents and if it is by day. But if it is by night, he will

---

[1] Something forbidden to Muslims.
[2] That is, his association with them.
[3] Reading *cursabit* instead of *bursabit*.
[4] A workman who made coins by striking metal discs with a hammer.

be of the major faith; and he will do good works; and he will be known and recognized in his own land, or in his community.

Chapter 3. *The Signification of Mars when it is in its own Domicile or in those of the other Planets.*

If Mars is in a domicile of Saturn, he will be a person of a tenacious disposition[1]; and he will have much anger. And if it is in Aquarius, he will be unlucky. And if it is in Capricorn, he will be bold spirited; and he will not be careless. And whatever actions he desires will come forth from [the action of] his own hands. And it will diminish his father's wealth; and his brothers will die.

If Mars is in a domicile of Jupiter, he will be associated in goodness with soldiers and masters of weapons. And if Jupiter is with it, he will be a great soldier, and a charming person; he will not be involved in evil actions. And if Jupiter makes a good aspect to it from a domicile of Mars, he will be a great person and like a count. And he will have an army; and his hand will [lie heavy] upon all his adversaries.

If Mars is in his own domicile, he will be a soldier and a boastful one. And he will be a geometrician[2] and lucky. And he will have much honor, and he will be married. And he will fall from a high place if Mars is in Aries and no benefic is aspecting it. And if it is in Scorpio, he will not be fearful; and he will be rich; [and] whatever actions he desires will come forth from his own hand. And it will be better if the birth is by night; and if it is by day, it will be evil, and he will be [a person] of evil speech.

If Mars is in the domicile of the Sun, he will have an illness from much heat[3]; but he will be lucky; and he will be afraid of wounds; and his death will be sudden; and he will be killed; and his father [will be killed] similarly in his old age.

---

[1]Reading *tenoris cordis* 'tenacious disposition' instead of *teneri cordis* 'tender disposition', which seems inappropriate for a combination of Mars and Saturn.

[2]Probably a surveyor or an engineer.

[3]Probably, one with a high fever.

If Mars is in a domicile of Venus, he will be a fornicator; and he will fornicate with his own relations; and he will be like a sodomite. He will have a wife from those with whom he will fornicate; and he will encounter evil from women. And if it is in Libra, he will be afraid of iron and fire and hidden places. And if it is in Taurus, he will be one of many children, and an evil person on account of his fornication.

If Mars is in a domicile of Mercury, he will be wise and knowledgeable; and he will encounter evils from actions that he does not desire. And he will have much wealth; and he will be traveling much; and he will encounter losses in his travels. And he will be an astronomer and a writer and a philosopher. And he will know how to free other things from their own proper places; and it will be when he will have little wealth and profit; and when his life will be from theft; and [his] actions will be evil for the most part.

If Mars is in the domicile of the Moon, he will serve princes; and he will suffer many evils; and his illness will be of various kinds in the belly and in a hidden place. And the illness of his mother will be prolonged. And he will have or give a great loss. And he will be afraid of sudden death.

Chapter 4. *The Signification of the Sun when it is in its own Domicile or in those of the other Planets.*

If the Sun is in a domicile of Saturn, it is good for him and his father; and if it is by day, he will be a person of great deeds. And he will be a person of an open face, or a stammerer, and a scoffer, or a keeper of the Sabbath,[1] and all of his actions will emerge from his own hands. And if it was by night, he will be against the evil of his father; and he will have little wealth; and he will be quickly angered; and he will be unsteady in his work; and he will change about from one thing to another.

If the Sun is in a domicile of Jupiter, it will be[an indication] for his goodness and elevation; he will have good actions and wis-

---

[1]That is, a Jew, and hence not a Muslim.

dom; and he will associate with princes; and he will be established over clean actions; and he will bring them into good; and he will be a good man, but esteemed in his own house and by his own kin. And if it is by day, he will associate with princes; and he will do evil, and it will be with the wife of his own father, and with the wives of his own close kin.

If the Sun is in a domicile of Mars, he will be in some way the ruination of his father; and he will encounter evil [accidents] from iron; and he will have a fear of sudden death, and of death in old age; and he will have pain in his bowels – and in his liver, if the Sun is in Scorpio. And if it is in Aries, he will be elevated and fortunate; and he will be honored during his whole life if it is by day; but if it is by night, these things will of lesser degree.

If the Sun is in its own domicile, and it is in an angle or in a succedent, he will be even more admired than a count; and he will be rich, and long-lived, and strong; and he will acquire great wealth from cities and towns. And if it is by night, he will be involved in foolishness, and [also] his father; and he will be separated from his father and his mother by travel.

If the Sun is in a domicile of Venus, he will have good things from women; and his good fortune will be from women; and he will open his own heart in extensive actions; and he will be one who judges dreams. And he will be recognized and known for the associates that he has been acquainted with. And he will be upright in good actions and in his travels.

If the Sun is in a domicile of Mercury, he will be an astronomer[1]; and he will have many horses; and he will be knowledgeable and fortunate; and he will be of good intelligence and with a better [than average] memory; and he will love scandals. And if it is by day, he will be more common. And if it is by night, he will have hindrance and trouble from phlegm and jaundice.

If the Sun is in the domicile of the Moon, the native will have

---

[1]Or, an astrologer.

joy and silliness and [he will have] little wealth; and he will be a bad worker. He will have more wealth in his youth; and he will have pain in his stomach and in hidden places [in his body]. And he will be involved with enchanters and conspirators and with those who will write briefs[1] to cure the sick.

Chapter 5. *The Signification of Venus.*

If Venus is in a domicile of Saturn, his evil will be from the taking of women; and he will love intercourse with old women and despised women; from which action, evils will be spoken about him. And all of his actions will be perfected, and he will be glad. And if it is by night, he will be involved in evil takings of women or marriages with them; and from that he will encounter evils and impediment; and he will see the death of his own wives.

If Venus is in a domicile of Jupiter, it is [an indication] for goodness and good fortune and for his elevation; and his wealth will be greater from women, or it will be from the action of some woman, or from the actions that he does with women—just as if he is the custodian of a lodging or an administrator or a governor. And if it is by night, it will be less [than that].

If Venus is in a domicile of Mars, he will encounter evils from enemies, and scandals; and he will associate with dishonorable slaves; and his marriage will turn out unpleasantly; and he will kill his own wife on account of jealousy.

If Venus is in the domicile of the Sun, he will be cheerful; and he will have a good life; and he will delight in dishonorable women; and he will love enjoyments and games; and men will say evil things about him. And he will see the greater part of his own wishes that he has in his heart.

If Venus is in her own domicile, it signifies many enjoyments, [and] the love of foolish women, from which he will have evil.

---

[1]Probably some sort of magical charm is meant.

Nevertheless, he will be fortunate in his own actions; and he will acquire good.

If Venus is in a domicile of Mercury, he will associate with greater men of the faith and with servant women; and [he will be involved] in actions that resemble those that are related to women, such as a painter, or a gilder, or something similar; and he will be fond of sexual intercourse.

If Venus is in the domicile of the Moon, he will have love in bad marriage with women, and [also] in enjoyment and games because of an error or from a desirable love. And he will have work involving collusion or crooked action.

Chapter 6. *The Signification of Mercury.*

If Mercury is in a domicile of Saturn, he will be wise in all his actions and an inventor of songs or praises, or he will be an astronomer[1] or a physician; or he will be unfortunate in getting wealth; and his speech will be serious; and he will associate with men of good credulity; and he will be manifestly honest.

If Mercury is in a domicile of Jupiter, he will associate with princes and businessmen; and he will have command or superintendence over princely actions; and he will be wise in his superintendence; a judge of good faith and credulity.

If Mercury is in a domicile of Mars, he will have a good understanding, and he will be knowledgeable; and he will have moderate wealth; or he will be a soldier; and he will write false edicts under the name of a judge or a prince; and he will be a liar; and from that he will encounter evils.

If Mercury is in the domicile of the Sun, he will have good association, and he will have good actions; and he will be an astronomer,[2] and knowledgeable about all [kinds of] actions; and his knowledge will increase every day; and he will be a person of good

---

[1] Or, an astrologer.
[2] Or, an astrologer.

intellect and memory; and he will be an inventor of profound and hidden sciences.

If Mercury is in a domicile of Venus, his heart will desire sexual intercourse; and he will regret it; and he will devote his life to good acting; and he will have many friends, and they will be like brothers. And he will like humorous things, such as lyric poetry and such like; and he portrays some ancient things well; and he will love the reason of numbers and the re-reading of books.

If Mercury is in his own domiciles, he will be irascible and touchy, and holding a grudge. And he will be a person knowing good things; and he will run a business; and he will be an inventor of profound and hidden sciences; and he will be an astronomer[1].

If Mercury is in the domicile of the Moon, he will be foolish; and he will travel much and be restless; and he will be a house builder; and he will get angry quickly and will be quickly soothed. And he will associate with greater men of the faith; and he will usually do his actions with [adequate] knowledge.

Chapter 7. *The Signification of the Moon in her own Domicile and in those of others.*

If the Moon is in a domicile of Saturn, he will have some evil, and so will his mother; and he will have pain from wind[2] and from his spleen; and evil things will be said about him. And if the Moon has little light, in his old age he will encounter pain from cold and from his kidneys. And it will be worse if it is by night.

If the Moon is in a domicile of Jupiter, it signifies greatness; and he will be born to goodness and good fortune; and he will be recognized among men. And he will lie with some man or woman who is not suitable, and with some prevarication; and he or she will be one of his close relations or some one close to him.

---

[1] Or, an astrologer.
[2] That is, from gas pains.

If the Moon is in a domicile of Mars, he will have a fickle head in his actions; and his mother will encounter evils; and he will be touchy and one who holds a grudge, especially in the case of scandals and wars. And he will associate with soldiers and armed robbers; and by night, he will associate with those going about for evil-doing.

If the Moon is in the domicile of the Sun, it signifies delight and a good life for the native; and he will associate with princes; and he will be famous; and he will have pain in his head and in his stomach, and this will be stronger if it is in the third sign. And it will be [at a time] when he has little wealth and little income.

If the Moon is in a domicile of Venus, it signifies delight; and his heart's desire to mate; and his marriage will take place with joy; and he will live well.

If the Moon is in a domicile of Mercury, he will have good intelligence; and he will be clean [in spirit]; and he will be good in faith; and he will desire women, boys, and girls; and he will be knowledgeable in his own actions.

If the Moon is in her own domicile, he will have great income; and he will be a person with honor; and he will associate with princes. And if the benefics are in aspect, it will be better; [but] if the malefics are in aspect, it will be worse.

Chapter 8. *The Signification of the Ruler of the ASC in the twelve Houses.*

When the ruler of the ASC is in the ASC, it will be good; and if a Planet is in aspect from the MC, he will encounter a great inheritance. And if it is in its own exaltation, it will be from a prince.

If the ruler of the ASC is in the 2nd, wealth will come into his hands, and he will lose it through one who is characteristic of the sign in which it is.

If the ruler of the ASC is in the 3rd, he will have elder brothers; and he will do much traveling; and if it aspects a benefic, he will have good faith or credulity; and he will be faithful. And if it aspects a malefic, he will be unfaithful.

If the ruler of the ASC is in the 4th, he will love his father and his own mother; and he will encounter impediment or lawsuits from greater men. And if the ruler of the ASC is in an honorable position, he will see income from his parents

If the ruler of the ASC is in the 5th, he will beget children while he is still in his own youth; and he will have personal worth from their birth.

If the ruler of the ASC is in the 6th, he will be involved in actions like those of a servant; and he will have much illness.

If the ruler of the ASC is in the 7th, he will encounter [good fortune] from some relation with women and from taking them.

If the ruler of the ASC is in the 8th, it signifies good from some old things, and from inheritance.

If the ruler of the ASC is in the 9th, he will be good in his faith and in his praying to God; and he will be involved in much travel; and he will excel in all knowledge.

If the ruler of the ASC is in the 10th, he will seek rulership, and he will encounter victory in greatness and elevation.

If the ruler of the ASC is in the 11th, he will flourish in finding faith, and in victory, and in [having] many friends; and he will have good fortune from them; and they will have good fortune from him.

If the ruler of the ASC is in the 12th, he will have many enemies and rivals; and he will be their ruler, or the one over them, or the victor if it is strong there and dignified. But if it is weak and debilitated, say the opposite.

Chapter 9. *The Signification of the Ruler of the Second House in the twelve Houses.*

If the ruler of the 2nd house is in the 1st, he will gain from his own actions; and he will be fortunate; and he will have wealth.

If the ruler of the 2nd is in the 2nd, it signifies a good life; and he will be rich.

If the ruler of the 2nd is in the 3rd, there will be contention between him and his brothers on account of wealth.

If the ruler of the 2nd is in the 4th, he will have wealth from his own parents.

If the ruler of the 2nd hose is in the 5th, he will have good fortune from his children; and they will have good fortune from him.

If the ruler of the 2nd is in the 6th, he will have good fortune from quadrupeds and slaves; and he will suffer illnesses from that.

If the ruler of the 2nd is in the 7th, he will be made wealthy by women and associates; and he will have profit from women.

If the ruler of the 2nd is in the 8th, he will find a great inheritance.

If the ruler of the 2nd is in the 9th, he will profit from travel; and he will not have profit in his location or his own habitation.

If the ruler of the 2nd is in the 10th, his life will be supported by princes and their servants.

If the ruler of the 2nd is in the 11th, he will have good fortune from friends; and they will have good fortune from him.

If the ruler of the 2nd is in the 12th, he will be a pauper; and he will do oppressive or evil actions; and he will not do them quickly And in his actions, many lies will be said; and he will be hindered from completing what he wants to do.

Chapter 10. *The Signification of the Ruler of the Third House in the twelve Houses.*

If the ruler of the 3rd house is in the 1st, he will see many good things from his brothers; and he will be rendered fortunate by his brothers and those close to him; and he will be a wanderer because he is often changed from one place to another place—from country to country.

If the ruler of the 3rd is in the 2nd, he will gain wealth from changing from one place to another place, and from the actions of his own brothers and those close to him.

If the ruler of the 3rd is in the 3rd, his brothers will be famous, so that he may come to them.

If the ruler of the 3rd is in the 4th, it signifies evil on his side from the some action of his own brothers.

If the ruler of the 3rd is in the 5th, his children will be called by the name of his brother; and his brothers will see good things from his own children.

If the ruler of the 3rd is in the 6th, it signifies evil for him and for his brothers.

If the ruler of the 3rd is in the 7th, his brothers will take away his wife.

If the ruler of the 3rd is in the 8th, it signifies evil and the death of his brothers in his own days.

If the ruler of the 3rd is in the 9th, his wife may not be of his own land and not from that of his brothers; and on account of women he will fall into traveling.

If the ruler of the 3rd is in the 10th, he will have few brothers and close relations; and he will be a wanderer from one place to another place.

If the ruler of the 3rd is in the 11th, his brothers will be good for him; and he will be made fortunate because of them.

If the ruler of the 3rd is in the 12th, enmity will fall between him and his brothers and close relations.

Chapter 11. *The Signification of the Ruler of the Fourth House in the twelve Houses.*

If the ruler of the 4th house is in the ASC, he will encounter evil from princes; and he will be a weak or evil person.

If the ruler of the 4th is in the 2nd, it signifies the good state of his father from some action of his.

If the ruler of the 4th is in the 3rd, it signifies the destruction of or the parting from his brothers with the wealth of his own father.

If the ruler of the 4th is in the 4th, his father will be famous and a person of a good life.

If the ruler of the 4th is in the 5th, his children will be six in number; and he will encounter discord or impediment resulting from them.

If the ruler of the 4th is in the 6th, his children will be like slaves or servants; and they will perform the services of servants.

If the ruler of the 4th is in the 7th, it signifies the goodness of his marriage.

If the ruler of the 4th is in the 8th, he will be made fortunate through inheritances and in something from old times.

If the ruler of the 4th is in the 9th, he will die while traveling; and his illnesses will mainly be in hidden places [in the body].

If the ruler of the 4th is in the 10th, it signifies the celebrity of his father with princes; and he will be involved in the actions of princes.

If the ruler of the 4th is in the 11th, he will have goodness from his friends.

If the ruler of the 4th is in the 12th, there will be evil involving his father and his close relations.

Chapter 12. *The Signification of the Ruler of the Fifth House in the twelve Houses.*

If the ruler of the 5th house is in the ASC, he will have good fortune from children and friends.

If the ruler of the 5th is in the 2nd, he will have brothers in his travels; and he will have profit from his own children.

If the ruler of the 5th is in the 3rd, he will have good fortune from women.

If the ruler of the 5th is in the 4th, his father will be rich in wealth and of long life; and he will see the children of his own children.

If the ruler of the 5th is in the 5th, his children will have goodness and a good life, and they will be famous.

If the ruler of the 5th is in the 6th, his children will have much fatigue, and they will have a life of weakness.

If the ruler of the 5th is in the 7th, he will get a wife who is older than he is; and he will have goodness and much wealth.

If the ruler of the 5th is in the 8th, his children will die during his own days; and he himself will find something like princely rule and elevation.

If the ruler of the 5th is in the 9th, he will not beget children in his own land.

If the ruler of the 5th is in the 10th, his children will have much fatigue; and he will have evil days; and he will not encounter any evils from princes.

If the ruler of the 5th is in the 11th, his children will have good fortune from princes.

If the ruler of the 5th is in the 12th, it signifies the enmity of his children towards him; and they will never rejoice together.

Chapter 13. *The Signification of the Ruler of the Sixth House in the twelve Houses.*

If the ruler of the 6th house is in the ASC, he will be unlucky; and he will be likened to slaves; and many days afterwards he will profit, and he will have good fortune from slaves and from quadrupeds.

If the ruler of the 6th is in the 2nd, he will be fortunate in medicine and from slaves and quadrupeds.

If the ruler of the 6th is in the 3rd, his brothers will oppose him; and one of them will desire evil and the death of another brother.

If the ruler of the 6th is in the 4th, his father will be an obscure person.

If the ruler of the 6th is in the 5th, it signifies evil for his children and servants.

If the ruler of the 6th is in the 6th, he will be a physician and a knowledgeable person, and he will know about herbs.

If the ruler of the 6th is in the 7th, his father will be made unfortunate by women.

If the ruler of the 6th is in the 8th, he will not have good fortune from slaves.

If the ruler of the 6th is in the 9th, he will be fortunate in buying quadrupeds; and he will have much illness while traveling.

If the ruler of the 6th is in the 10th, he will have modest wealth; and he will have bad love[1] from princes.

If the ruler of the 6th is in the 11th, he will be a pauper and a person with a bad life.

If the ruler of the 6th is in the 12th, he will feel sorrows because of quadrupeds and slaves; and he will never be happy.

Chapter 14. *The Signification of the Ruler of the Seventh House in the twelve Houses.*

If the ruler of the 7th house is in the ASC, he will be very quarrelsome; and [he will do] better in the actions of women.

If the ruler of the 7th is in the 2nd, it signifies his quarrels over the things of women.

If the ruler of the 7th is in the 3rd, it signifies the enmity of the Native with his brothers.

---

[1]That is, hatred.

If the ruler of the 7th is in the 4th, [it signifies] his enmity with his father and his brothers.

If the ruler of the 7th is in the 5th, [it signifies] his enmity with his children.

If the ruler of the 7th is in the 6th, he will have evil because of women and servants.

If the ruler of the 7th is in the 7th, it signifies his good condition from marriage, and the understanding of his wives.

If the ruler of the 7th is in the 8th, he will get a wife, and she will die, and he will get her wealth.

If the ruler of the 7th is in the 9th, he will get a wife from a good family or from a princely race.

If the ruler of the 7th is in the 10th, he will get a wife who is fortunate and of a good life, and she will be elevated.

If the ruler of the 7th is in the 11th, it signifies his good condition [resulting] from marriage, and the good condition of his wives.

If the ruler of the 7th is in the 12th, he will get marriage or a wife from evil men, and he will never be happy with another.

Chapter 15. *The Signification of the ruler of the Eighth House [in the twelve Houses].*

If the ruler of the 8th house is in the ASC, he will be weak in body and spirit.

If the ruler of the 8th is in the 2nd, he will find wealth from an inheritance.

If the ruler of the 8th is in the 3rd, he will be cheerful because of some occurrence with his female relatives.

If the ruler of the 8th is in the 4th, it signifies the ruin of his own father and his worthlessness.

If the ruler of the 8th is in the 5th, his children will die.

If the ruler of the 8th is in the 6th, he will always be healthy.[1]

If the ruler of the 8th is in the 7th, he will squander the inheritances of women; and his wives will be a loss to him in traveling.

If the ruler of the 8th is in the 8th, he will be of a mind to gain wealth, and it will occur.

If the ruler of the 8th is in the 9th, it signifies the same thing.

If the ruler of the 8th is in the 10th, in his childhood he will try to have power over men; and he will not have it in that time of life.

If the ruler of the 8th is in the 11th, he will be a known person; and he will use foul or evil words.

If the ruler of the 8th is in the 12th, he will have few enemies; [but] his slaves will kill him.

Chapter 16. *The Signification of the Ruler of the Ninth House in the twelve Houses.*

If the ruler of the 9th house is in the ASC, he will make many journeys; and he will be knowledgeable and too miserly.

If the ruler of the 9th is in the 2nd, he will encounter cheer from an inheritance; and he will be generous.

If the ruler of the 9th is in the 3rd, his brothers will make marriages while traveling.

If the ruler of the 9th is in the 4th, his father will be worthless.

If the ruler of the 9th is in the 5th, he will have much travel and many children.

If the ruler of the 9th is in the 6th, he will get sick while traveling.

If the ruler of the 9th is in the 7th, he will make foreign mar-

---

[1]Considering the nature of the two houses, this seems to be an optimistic prediction.

riages.

If the ruler of the 9th is in the 8th, [it signifies] the same thing.

If the ruler of the 9th is in the 9th, he will be involved in travel and in the path of his own father; and he will be a good worker; and he will have good faith.

If the ruler of the 9th is in the 10th, in his travel he will find something like a rulership, and he will profit from something like that.

If the ruler of the 9th is in the 11th, his goodness will be in travel, and he will have a long life.

If the ruler of the 9th is in the 12th, he will have bad credulity or faith; and in traveling he will see impediment from his friends.

Chapter 17. *The Signification of the Ruler of the Tenth House in the twelve Houses.*

If the ruler of the 10th house is in the ASC, it signifies his [receiving] goodness from princes; and he will be famous.

If the ruler of the 10th is in the 2nd, he will assemble his wealth from the action of a prince.

If the ruler of the 10th is in the 3rd, it signifies the good condition of his brothers and sisters.

If the ruler of the 10th is in the 4th, his father will be well known for his goodness.

If the ruler of the 10th is in the 5th, it rather indicates the illness and bad condition of his children.

If the ruler of the 10th is in the 6th, he will make a marriage with elder relatives of princes.

[The signification of the ruler of the 10th in the 7th is missing.]

If the ruler of the 10th is in the 8th, it rather indicates the good condition of his wives from it.

[The signification of the ruler of the 10th in the 9th is missing.]

If the ruler of the 10th is in the 10th, it signifies the stability of his rulership.

If the ruler of the 10th is in the 11th, it signifies his rulership in his own childhood.[1]

If the ruler of the 10th is in the 12th, it will make enmity with princes; and he will always be at discord with princes.

Chapter 18. *The Signification of the Ruler of the 11th in the twelve Houses.*

If the ruler of the 11th is in the ASC, it will show good association with men; and he will have many friends.

If the ruler of the 11th is in the 2nd, it signifies his good condition from friends.

If the ruler of the 11th is in the 3rd, he will be well thought of by his brothers and sisters.

If the ruler of the 11th is in the 4th, it signifies the destruction of his father and his own evil condition.[2]

If the ruler of the 11th is in the 5th, there will be good in his own household and in his own children.

If the ruler of the 11th is in the 6th, he will delight in evil and foul women.

If the ruler of the 11th is in the 7th, it signifies his own good condition and that of his wives and children.

If the ruler of the 11th is in the 8th, it signifies the destruction of his neighbors and friends.

If the ruler of the 11th is in the 9th, he will make marriages while traveling or with foreign women.

---

[1]There have been some historical instances of small children becoming nominal kings or rulers.
[2]The 11th is the 8th house from the 4th.

If the ruler of the 11th is in the 10th, his friends will encounter good conditions from him.

If the ruler of the 11th is in the 11th, he will be honored and rich and elevated.

If the ruler of the 11th is in the 12th, he will be unlucky and [will have] a bad life.

Chapter 19. *The Signification of the Ruler of the 12th in the twelve Houses.*

If the ruler of the 12th house is in the ASC, he will be unlucky and he will have a bad life. He will have many enemies; and all of them will be above him.

If the ruler of the 12th is in the 2nd, he will have little wealth, and he will be slack in his actions.

If the ruler of the 12th is in the 3rd, he will have enmity with his brothers and with his neighbors.

If the ruler of the 12th is in the 4th, it signifies evil and little travel for his father.

If the ruler of the 12th is in the 5th, it signifies evil for his children.

If the ruler of the 12th is in the 6th, it signifies evil for his quadrupeds, his slaves, his servants, and his hirelings.

If the ruler of the 12th is in the 7th, it signifies evil for his wives and their mutual enmities.

If the ruler of the 12th is in the 8th, his enemy will work to kill him.

If the ruler of the 12th is in the 9th, he will have bad faith.

If the ruler of the 12th is in the 10th, he will see losses and impediments from princes.

If the ruler of the 12th is in the 11th, he will have a small inheritance, and few friends, and many enemies.

If the ruler of the 12th is in the 12th, he will not fear from enemies and adversaries.

Chapter 20. *The Signification of Saturn when it is in its own Terms or in those of the other Planets in the Nativity.*

If Saturn is in its own terms, it bestows greatness and many
things on the Native, and wealth from many [different] things. But
he will be weak; and he will have his power from greater men, and
from being in their service, and in the service of religious persons.
And he will gain everything because of his faith; and he will be
very rich; and everyone will come to him for counsel about various
matters. And if the benefics aspect it, all of the above said will be
increased; and if the malefics aspect it, they will be decreased.

But if Saturn is in the terms of Jupiter, the Native will have
many things; but in his youth he will lose and squander everything,
and he will be sad; but he will have a great name – both he and his
house. And his periods of servitude will be moderate up to his 38th
year; and thereafter he will rejoice in his own offspring. And at that
time he will see what he has wanted, and had only thought about
before; and the native will see many good things. And in that
house where he will be born, there will be a man having a defect in
his eye or an illness; and his wealth will be greater. And after he
has passed his 28th year, the servitudes of the previously mentioned Native will be good; and he will change many things; and
he will encounter great servitudes. And if a benefic aspects it from
its own exaltation, it will increase the things said above.

If Saturn is in the terms of Mars, his road is demonstrated thus.
Seeing that the Native's parents are foreigners and paupers—this
Native will squander and tear apart their wealth. And he will kill
those who closely fawn upon him; or with iron he will beat some
brother, whom a physician will heal. And he will find discord with
his first wife. And after the years of this Planet have passed by in
his nativity and he is made an old man, he will pass into the service
of religious persons; and many sorrows will find him; but if the
benefics are in aspect, he will be set free.

If Saturn is in the terms of Venus, it is seen thus. Seeing that the Native will have much illness in his youth; and his father will have died along with his mother; and he will have children from two wives; and he will encounter lawsuits for his wives. And at the end he will rejoice; and he will gather together the children of his own close relations; and pain will appear in his testicles, so that he is unable to lie with a woman. And he will see plenty of mediocrity and poverty until the years of this Planet have passed by; and afterwards he will rejoice with his close relations and with his own children; and he will be in the first place. And if the benefics are in aspect, he will get a wife with much wealth.

If Saturn is in the terms of Mercury, it seems that the Native will encounter a lawsuit for women; and he will see the death of children; and many days will pass by, and his wife will not become pregnant; and afterwards she will bear a daughter, who will live until he gives her a husband; and he will see her marriage, and he will beget sons and daughters. And he will appear great in the eyes of men, and they will not approach him; and some of them will have a great name; and men will honor him for the actions of his hands; and they will hold him [to be] good. And he will encounter a lawsuit by princes or greater men; and he will be made destitute, so that he has nothing; and he will be captured as booty. But if the benefics are in aspect, he will be liberated.

Chapter 21. *The Signification of Jupiter in his own Terms or in those of others.*

If Jupiter is in his own terms, the Native will be in charge of great services; and he will [live to] see the children of his own children. And when Jupiter has entered into his own terms, he will find wealth; and greater men will rely upon him; and there is not another hand above his own hand in his service; and he will find wealth from business transactions; and he will take care of the house of his own father; and he will comfort and aid him.[1]

---

[1] Reading *eum* 'him' instead of *eam* 'her' or 'it' (the house).

If Jupiter is in the terms of Saturn, he will have a pain in his head; and he will be captured by enemies; and with money he will be ransomed from them; and he will find various things and advantage from business transactions; and his enemies will not have strength; and he will know, or he will find out, how to add to the secrets of women; and he will be happy with his wife and his children. And whenever Jupiter enters the terms of Saturn, he will want to look out carefully at his own assets. And if benefics are aspecting it, he will be freed from the above said things. And if that benefic is in its own domicile, its benefits will be plain to see; and he will find truth from greater men. The usefulness or the work of his ministers will not be uniform through seven years.

If Jupiter is in the terms of Mars he will encounter much malice; and he will be captured by enemies; and he will die a bad death. And he will be involved in doing something with iron; and his son will die; and he himself will die before his son is born. And if benefics aspect it, the evils will be lessened; and he will beget a son in his old age; and he will [live to] see his death.

If Jupiter is in the terms of Venus, he will be handsome, serious and honorable; and he will get an honorable wife. And he will be in charge of services for greater men; and his usefulness and fortune will be from business transactions. And he will be in charge of male and female servants, who will honor him as their master; and men will speak well of him and after him. And he will be taking care of household goods in [the houses of men of] great wealth; or he will be in charge of great services guarding household goods. And he will always be happy; and he will be religious around the end of his life.

If Jupiter is in the terms of Mercury, he will want to know the books of various religions and beliefs; and men will like him and esteem him highly. And he will find good fortune from some situation with women; or from some accident or action he will have his utility. And he will not be a pauper; and he will be in charge of services of belief; and he will be in charge of the services of princes, just like a prince; and he will be in charge of military camps; and he will have large country-houses. And he will be just, honorable, and religious; and the end of his work will always be useful. And if it is in its own domicile, it will increase all the aforesaid things.

Chapter 22. *The Signification of Mars in his own Terms and in those of others.*

If Mars is in his own terms, he will be a companion of soldiers for the duration of the years; and he will be made like a great person; and men will be grateful to him; and they will say good things about him. And his life will encounter a medium amount of discord and lawsuits; and the king will be angry with him; but he will be freed from him; and he will find pain from haste and from wearing arms, and because he stands in the middle of a battle. And if a benefic aspects it, he will find a position of importance; and kings will be from him and after him; or they will say good words about him; and he will be in charge of great services and great things; and he will have many enemies. And the end of his works and his life will be praiseworthy. And he will do something malicious to his own wife.

If Mars is in the terms of Saturn, he will see the death of his own children and his close relatives. And he will drink poisons or something toxic. and if a benefic aspects it, he will be freed; but it will destroy the wealth of his own father; and he will encounter a lawsuit in his old age; and he will go into places in which something maliciousn will rise up against him. And whenever Mars enters into the terms of Saturn, he will encounter a lawsuit, for however long the forces of the year will last. And then much wealth will come into his hands; and he will beget children and rejoice; and afterwards he will experience troubles, and from them many natives will die a sudden death.

If Mars is in the terms of Jupiter, much wealth will come into his hands; and [yet] he will find pain and trouble and illness, and he will be made stupid or mindless. And if he has a wife, he will not impregnate her. And he will make many journeys; and it will destroy all of his own wealth; and he will encounter a lawsuit and pain because of the occurrence of blasphemies, in which he did not sin; and he will enter into scandal and quarrels; and if a benefic aspects it, he will find elevation, [but] if a malefic aspects it, he will encounter humiliation.

If Mars is in the terms of Venus, he will have an evil life from something relating to women; and he will get a wife from some sinful event; and he will be caught in sinful intercourse or in fornication; and he will get prostitutes, and he will have them; and many days will pass. And his works will not be good, and he will do nothing good with his own wife and with his children, since his children that he will beget will die young. Then, from the evil path that he was in, he will be converted, and he will spend much money on women. And he will not remain in his own faith; and he will become insane from something involving women. And he will be captured and given as booty. And he will make many travels; and he will get a wife unequal [in status] and unlike him.

And if Mars is in a domicile of Venus, whatever will happen to him of good or evil will be mixed. But whenever Mars enter into the terms of Venus, he wants to make progress or to see his own personal things.

If Mars is in the terms of Mercury, he will be a commissary,[1] or he will have some similar office, [and he will do] many different things; and no good will be spoken of him and of everything that he does.Enemies will make accusations against him; and [yet] he will have many good results from the duties that he performs; and he is not alone in his own duties. And he is always angry with his own wife and children. And men look for someone else in place of him, and are turned away from him. And if a benefic does aspect Mars, he will be freed from all these evils.

Chapter 23. *The Signification of the Sun in the Terms of others.*

If the Sun is in the terms of Saturn, he will live long and will be fortunate. And if he has brothers, they will be similar. And he will

---

[1]Someone who carries out the orders of a superior.

be like a prince in the houses of kings, or a judge, and all of his services will be out in the open. And he will rejoice in his children.

If the Sun is in the terms of Jupiter, he will be like a prince; and he will be clothed in gold and silver; and he will fear God and adore Him much. Or he will be a great businessman; and the end of his services will be good.

If the Sun is in the terms of Mars, he will be ardent in spirit; and he will get angry quickly; and he will be fortunate; and he will take a trip on the sea; and from some collision with iron, he will encounter discord and a bad illness. And if any of the malefics aspects the Sun, he will be the doorkeeper of some house [of worship] in which prayer is given; or he will be a sort of fast tradesman. And if a benefic aspects it, he will be freed from those things.

If the Sun is in the terms of Venus, he will always be cheerful, and he will love women; and he will be in many services [of women]; and he will look for or get a wife from among his close kin. And he will be in the place of those who are greater in faith; and he will always be in that place, and he will be close to it; and he will do good works, from which he will find the reward of those who travel for God; and he will acquire [some knowledge] of the sciences; and wherever he goes, his works will be good; and his wealth will be abundant.

If the Sun is in the terms of Mercury, his [profession in] life will be from writing; and he will be like a physician; and he will be fortunate, and one who says right things; or he will be a lawyer; and he will be close to kings.

Chapter 24. *The Signification of Venus in her own Terms or in those of others.*

If Venus is in her own terms, he will have joy from women and children; he will be a sort of counselor; and he will be like a ruler over servants and maidservants; and he will be good-hearted towards them; and he will be [situated] in a place of religious men or priests; and he will be like a Bishop in charge of priests; and he will be highly esteemed wherever he is. And he will be good to his parents; and he will have good children, who will be strong. And whenever Venus enters into her own terms, his services will be good, and the laity esteem him highly.

If Venus is in the terms of Saturn, he will find a pain in the head from some relation with women; and he will seek and acquire a wife who is talkative, irascible, and stubborn. And he will stay many days without a wife; and afterwards he will get an old woman or one of lower class than himself, and a common one, and she will see a short old age. And whenever Venus enters into the terms of Saturn, he will be made clean, and he will do foul or evil things, And if a benefic and also a malefic aspects Venus, whatever comes to him will be a mixture of good and evil.

If Venus is in the terms of Jupiter, he will be wise, and he will have joy in all the work that he does; and he will have a great inheritance and varied possessions. And he will be bold and firm-hearted, famous and well-known; and he will be a teacher in religious places, known for his principles and rules. And his wife will be good and wise; and the end of his work will be good and praiseworthy.

If Venus is in the terms of Mars, he will have pain in taking women; and he will be a fornicator; and he will be skilled in fornication. And he will find pain from some experience with a serving maid or a slave, and from a lawsuit made by women. And he will find pain in the head from some experience with his freedmen, because they will be rustics. Moreover, he will have a lawsuit from [something related to] iron; and he will have pain whenever he tells many lies; and his fortune will be greater from robbery; and his death will be due to some encounter with a woman.

And whenever Venus enters into the terms of Mars, he will want to be cleansed of evils as it were. And if Venus is in her own domicile, whatever comes to him will be a mixture of good and evil.

If Venus is in the terms of Mercury, he will see joy from his wife and offspring; and he will get a wife, from whom he will see many good things. And he will rejoice from an experience with joking activities. And he will get wealth and governorship from kings; and he will be in charge of servants and maid-servants; and he will have governorship over mobs. And he will be a good writer; and one who will know something good about everything; and he will be highly honored; and he will be like a teacher and judge in his own camp; and his works will be plain to all; and they will listen to him in everything that he teaches. And if there are any who do any evil to him, they will find damage and evil.

And if Venus is in a common sign, he will find a great dignity; and he will pass his life in joy through many days. And if a malefic aspects Venus, it will diminish the above said things.

Chapter. 25. *The Signification of Mercury in his own Terms or in those of others.*

If Mercury is in his own terms, he will be highly-placed, and he will have governorship over the place where they write documents. And he will always be involved in travel; he will never be a pauper; he will have a great name; he will be a member of a governing body; and he will seek [to know] the sciences; and he will be light-hearted and not serious; and he will teach men fluency; and he will be a writer for princes or kings; and he will gather together wealth upon wealth; and the mob will rejoice in him, because he will give benefits to them. And he will always be in good condition because of his knowledge; and he will see good dreams. Moreover, he will be made sad by some event relating to women; and afterwards he will rejoice.

If Mercury is in the terms of Saturn, he will be pleasing for his own virtue; and enmity will occur between him and his brothers; and he will see the death of his own brothers; and many days will pass by; and his wife will be impregnated; and it will be of less fortune for women. And he will spend many days in travel; and he will be made rich; and afterwards he will find loss. And a close relation will have some scandal with him; and they will go in a ceremonial manner to the prince; but his hand will be stronger than their hands; and he will be ill from hidden causes; and he will spend years in joy and goodness.

And whenever Mercury enters into the terms of Saturn, he will want to be purified.

If Mercury is in the terms of Jupiter, he will be knowledgeable and a good counselor and a merchant; and he will be elevated in rank; and he will have a great name; and he will be a sort of ruler of common people and illiterate ones for their own good; and he will be in charge of many things, and in charge of the services of princes and elders. And a long life will pass by for him in common circumstances, until his father has lived [his life]. And men want to serve his offspring; and his sons and daughters will be mercurial types; and his enemies will be weak before him.

If Mercury is in the terms of Mars, he will have much greed, from which pain and discord always arise for him; and his actions will not be good; and he will encounter loss and headache from some occurrence with women; and his understanding will deteriorate; and afterwards he will lie in intercourse with his own offspring. And when Mercury is in his own domicile, the above said things will be of lesser severity; and he is always wishing to be purified whenever Mercury enters the terms of Mars.

If Mercury is in the terms of Venus, he will be a ruler of elders; and he will be pleasant to his children and his own wife. And he will be rich and a counselor of his own associates; and he will always be pleasant in his own actions, [while] having command of servants, slaves, and foreigners. And if he is of the faith of his elders, he will be knowledgeable in all his action; and he will be in charge of services of princes and of religious houses. And he will die in his own home; and he will flee from fear in his own spirit.

And if Mercury is in his own domicile, his days will pass in exaltation and goodness. And if Mercury is in his own fall, his works will be middling; and he will know the arts; and if malefics are in aspect, he is one of those who do not know the arts.

Chapter 26. *The Signification of the Moon in the terms of others.*

If the Moon is in the terms of Saturn, he will encounter a lawsuit from women and from his own offspring. And he will not get a wife until the first year of Saturn has passed. And whatever comes into his hands will be destroyed until Saturn has completely run through the zodiac; and afterwards much wealth will come into his hands; and he will enjoy his wife and children; and his life will pass along just as is proper.

If the Moon is in the terms of Jupiter, his fortune will be greater from trade and travel; and he will encounter a lawsuit; and his children will be honored in his own days. And his wealth will increase just as his days increase; and his life will extend to many days in old age; and his life will always be good.

If the Moon is in the terms of Mars, he will be irascible and eager to anger; and his actions will be from fire and iron. And he will encounter discord and loss from weapons and quadrupeds, or from wild animals. And if a benefic is in aspect, he will be freed from all the above said things.

If the Moon is in the terms of Venus, he will be good, and he will have elevation; and from some incident of fornication he will get a wife; and he will act insolently in his own house; and a separation will come between them. And he will pass over that and get children from two wives; and he will get a wife unlike himself. And he will find much wealth without litigation; and he will have honor from princes.

If the Moon is in the terms of Mercury, he will be a good writer; and he will have many thoughts and desires in his own heart; and from that same situation he will find usefulness; and he will be a government man, and one placed over the teaching of princes. And writers will hold him to be great and dear; and he will be involved in services relating to the mob. And he will have good sense and counsel; and the end of his action will be good, if God wills.

INDEX OF PERSONS

BIBLIOGRAPHY

Firmicus Maternus, Julius
Matheseos Libri VIII.
ed. by W. Kroll, F. Skutsch, and K. Ziegler
Leipzig: B. G. Teubner Verlagsgesellschaft, 1968. 2nd ed. 2
vols.

Mâshâ⁾allâh
Incipit Messahalla super significationibus planetarum
in nativitate...
edited by Joachim Heller
Nürnberg: Johannes Montanus & Ulricus Neuberus, 1549.

al-Nadîm
The Fihrist of al-Nadîm.
edited and translated by Bayard Dodge
New York and London: Columbia University Press, 1970. 2
vols.

MÂSHÂ'ALLÂH

THE EPISTLE ON THE CONJUNCTIONS OF THE PLANETS

Translated from the Twelfth Century Latin Version
of John of Seville

by

JAMES HERSCHEL HOLDEN, M.A.
Fellow of the American Federation of Astrologers

Contents

TRANSLATOR'S PREFACE

Mâshâ⟩allâh was the adopted Muslim name of the Jewish astrologer Mîshâ ibn Athrâ from Basra, Iraq, who converted to Islam and became one of the greatest Arabian[1] astrologers. He was born about 730 A.D. and lived until about 815. He was one of the astrological consultants employed by the Caliph al-Manṣûr (679-777) to make an election for the founding of the new city of Baghdad in 762.[2] Al-Nadîm[3] says this about Mâshâ⟩allâh: "He was a man of distinction and during his period the leading person for the science of judgments of the stars."

He was probably acquainted with the Greek astrologer Theophilus (d. 777), who seems to have been the first prominent Arabian astrologer. Theophilus wrote several books on astrology that survive in Greek versions, but the Arabic versions were unknown to the Twelfth Century Translators, who turned much Arabian astrology into Latin and sparked the recovery of astrology in Western Europe.

Mâshâ⟩allâh thus became the earliest Arabian astrologer whose works were known in the West. He wrote on a variety of subjects and was considered by both later Arabian astrologers and European astrologers to be a prime authority. His short *Epistle on the*

---

[1]By *Arabian*, I mean all those, of whatever ethnic group, who wrote in the Arabic language.
[2]See my paper "The Foundation Chart of Baghdad" in *Today's Astrologer* Vol. 65, No. 3 (March 2, 2003): 9-10 & 29.
[3]See the priceless catalogue of Arabic literature as it existed at the end of the 10th century, *The Fihrist of al-Nadîm* edited and translated by Bayard Dodge (New York and London: Columbia Univerity Press, 1970. 2 vols.), II, p. 650.

Conjunctions of the Planets was translated into Latin by John of Seville and is described as *Epistola Messahallah in rebus eclipsis Lune et in coniunctionibus planetarum ac revolutionibus annorum breviter elucidata* 'Mâshâ'allâh's Epistle on things about Eclipses of the Moon and the Conjunctions of the Planets and the Revolutions of Years briefly elucidated'. The text gives the impression of having been edited by someone besides the author, since the chapters begin with the phrase, "Mâshâ'allâh said."

The first edition of this book was published in 1493 by Bonetus Locatellus at Venice in an omnibus edition of astrological works. I have used a xerox copy of the Latin text included in that edition. The text is neatly printed in two columns of abbreviated Latin on folios 148^r – 149^r.

James H. Holden
31 October 2007

The Epistle on the Conjunction of the Planets.

Chapter 1. *An Account of the Circle and the Stars and how they act in this Age.*

Mâshâ'allâh said, the Highest Lord made the Earth in the likeness of a sphere; and He made a higher circle spinning around it; and He put the Earth fixed and immobile in the middle of the circle, neither inclining to the right nor to the left. And He put four moving elements; and He made them to be moved by the motion of the seven Planets. But the Head of the Dragon[1] and the signs and all the stars share with the seven Planets in their own actions and natures.

Similar, therefore, is the action of the planets on this world of magnetic stone and iron, because just as the iron is attracted by that stone through a known distance, so every creature and all things that are on the face of the Earth are brought about by the motion of the Planets, and by all the things that are above the earth, such as crops and the good fortune or impediment of animals; things also that are fitting or destructive are made by the motions of the Planets, and their actions, of which thing the greatest signification is the diversity of men in their own being, and in their fortunes and misfortunes.

And because we see certain rational persons to be deprived of goods, but some stupid persons to be enjoying them, even when this does not have any cause signifying it—so that fortune and

---

[1]The Moon's North Node.

misfortune are made without any choice or will of their own, for those who are experiencing fortunate conditions and unfortunate conditions. And this situation by the will of God is the action of the Planets and their [influence on] fortune and misfortune.

Chapter 2. *The Diversity of the Imprints of the Action of the Stars on the Regions of Earth.*

Know that the actions of the Planets are diverse according to the diversity of the climes, because in some climes some Planets are made fortunate, and some are made evil in another clime in different ways; and therefore, every rational person must understand the characteristics of the climes and the regions; such as the region of Ethiopia in which heat scorches; and the land of the Slavs, with whom cold is everlasting; and the Planets that signified for the citizens of Ethiopia a superfluity of cold tempers their air to a favorable [degree]; but this same cold signifies for the Slavs a congealing of their air, and their habitation will perish.

And on account of this, knowledge of the character of the climes and regions and the airs is necessary. And know that the knowledge of the stars is very important, and that it can be better known from this—namely, that everything is universal and plural, as are the Revolutions of the years and eclipses. And know the significations of all of these. And this is not [possible] except by the recognition of the natures of the signs, and whatever each one of them signifies both about regions and provinces and all things. And we have already said this in our [other] books; but now we may say a part of these things more briefly. And now we begin with the aid of God.

Chapter 3. *The Natures of the Signs.*

The signs are 12 [in number]; in each sign there are also 30 degrees; and in each degree there are 60 minutes; and in each minute 60 seconds; and so on down to the quantity of a point; that is, down to infinity. And these are their names: Aries, Taurus, etc.; and they have significations over fire, and air, water, and earth. For three of them are fire: Aries, namely; Leo and Sagittarius; and three are earth: Taurus, Virgo, Capricorn; and three are air: Gemini, Libra, Aquarius; and three are water: Cancer, Scorpio, and Pisces. For the fire signs are hot, and the water signs cold; the earth signs are also cold, and the air signs are hot.

And know that all the hot signs are masculine, and the cold ones feminine; and all the masculine ones are diurnal, and the feminine ones are nocturnal. There are also four mobile signs, namely those in which the times[1] [of the year] are moved, which are Aries, Cancer, Libra, and Capricorn. And four fixed ones, in which the time is fixed, which are Taurus, Leo, Scorpio, and Aquarius. There are also four that are bicorporeal or common, namely those in which two times are combined; these are Gemini, Virgo, Sagittarius, and Pisces. Understand that these are the natures of the signs!

Chapter 4. *The Revolution of Years.*

When you want to know what may happen in the World with regard to rains and winds, etc., establish the ASC at the hour of the Ingress of the Sun into the first point of Aries; and put in the seven Planets at that same hour; and in the figure you have made, consider which of them rules it. Which, if it is a benefic it will make the time suitable; but if it is a malefic or if it is impeded—it will be a corrupted World.

And know that when many of the Planets are conjoined in water signs in the Revolution of the Year, they will signify a multitude of rains; and in the fire signs, they will signify an excess of heat and dryness or the barrenness of the land; and in air signs, they will signify a multitude of winds; and in the earth signs, they will signify cold and snows. And similarly, in the quarters of the year, when there are Planets in cold places, they will signify severity of cold and diminution of heat.

Know that when Mars and Saturn rule the Revolution, and the benefics do not aspect them, they will signify a multitude of wars

---

[1]That is, the *seasons*.

and the destruction of the World; so also when there is a malefic ruler of the quarter of summer; and when Mercury is in some of the houses, it will signify a multitude of rains and pestilences. And know that the severity of the dryness, and the barrenness of the land in the want of grain, does not occur unless it is from a conjunction of the Planets in fire signs. Understand this, and prove it according to what I have said to you, and you will find it [to be so]!

Chapter 5. *The Eclipse of the Moon and its Signification.*

Mâshâ'allâh said, you ought to consider the eclipses of the year, both lunar and solar, and you ought to know the ASC of mid-eclipse and the Planet that rules that ASC and its figure. Which, if it is a malefic, it will signify impediment and destruction; but if it is a benefic, it will signify agreeable conditions. And know that an eclipse of the Moon, when it is in cold signs, signifies severity of cold, and in water signs an excess of rains if it is appropriate to the time, i.e. in winter time; but if it is summer, it signifies a temperate condition of the air.

Understand and prove thus the rest. You should also understand that when benefics aspect the Moon and receive her, there will be a good and advantageous signification for those things that it signified.

Chapter 6. *Changes of the Weather [signified] by Changes of the Planets.*

Mâshâ'allâh said, when you want to know in advance the variety of the time with regard to the diverse things of the corruptible World, know the signs of the heavy Planets—namely, whether they are hot or cold—and if they are hot signs, they will signify heat in the summer and mildness of the air in the winter, and [if they are cold signs, cold in the winter and] mildness in the summer. And similarly, when the Planets are conjoined in water signs, it signifies excessive rains and corruption of the air by those same Planets in the winter, and mildness of the air and a multitude of moisture in the summer. And appraise [the weather] according to that, because you will not err. Moreover, the heavy Planets are Saturn, Jupiter, and Mars.

You ought also to couple them with [their relationship to] the Sun. Know that the heavy Planets, when they are [under the Sun beams], will signify dryness in the direction of any region as well as barrenness of the land; but when they are truly elongated from the Sun, they signify a multitude of rains. I want it to be understood by closeness [to mean] when they are in the northern signs, and by distance when they are in the southern ones. Know also that the heavy Planets, when they are all oriental, will signify a multitude of rains in the winter and mildness of the air in the summer. And similarly, in their rising[1] they signify an advantageous state of the air in the winter and excessive dryness in the summer.

Chapter 7. *The Eclipse of the Sun and its Signification.*

Mâshâ'allâh said: know that in an eclipse of the Sun, nothing can be done without some great happening being signified according to the quantity of that eclipse's condition,[2] i.e. as it is being made from a quarter of the body of the Sun and above [that amount]. Moreover, the knowledge of those things that happen from the eclipse of the Sun is obtained when you know the ASC of the middle of the eclipse, and the Planets that are ruling the figure of the eclipse. But if they were malefics, they will signify evil and detriment, and the death of Kings and rich persons; and if they are benefics, they will signify good fortune and advantage for the essence of things.

And you may know that when an eclipse of the Sun is in Aries, it will signify the demise of kings and rich persons, and dryness or barrenness of the land, and famine; and so in the rest of the fire signs. But in water signs, it will signify a multitude of rains and detriment from them.

Understand too that when the benefics are in aspect, they dimin-

---

[1]That is, when they are *oriental*.
[2]Its *magnitude*, as the astronomers call it.

ish the evil, but when the malefics are in aspect, they will amplify that evil and will diminish the good fortune. Know also that when the Sun or the Moon is Hyleg or the *alcochoden*[1] of any one and is obscured, they will also signify great danger or serious illness for the one that is [represented by] the Hyleg or the *alcochoden* unless the benefics are in aspect.

Chapter 8. *The Conjunction of all the Planets and their Effects.*

Mâshâʾallâh said, the conjunction of the Planets signifies the accidents of this World and the things [in it] that are thus considered at the time of the conjunction of both the higher Planets and the lower ones, because the benefics signify good fortune and good effects if they rule over the figure of the conjunction; but if the malefics are ruling, they will signify evil and evil effects.

You will also know that when they are conjoined in any one of the signs, they will signify much detriment according to the substance of that same sign. That is, if it is conjoined in water signs, it will signify a detriment from rain; and so in the rest of the signs. But if they are conjoined in feminine signs, they will signify pestilence and the death of animals of the feminine sex; and the same thing is said about masculine signs [and animals of the masculine sex].

And know that conjunctions and eclipses of the Lights, when they are in fixed signs will signify the durability of evil and its detriment; and if they are in mobile signs, they will signify little durability of the evil and its detriment; but if they are in common signs, they will signify evil moderately; and you may say the same thing about good!

Chapter 9. *The Conjunction of the Superior Planets.*

Mâshâʾallâh said, know that great and marvelous things happen from the conjunction of the superior Planets, and this is done be-

---

[1]Variously spelled in Latin, it is from the Arabic *al-kadkhudâh*, which is from a Persian word used to translate the Greek *oikodespotês* 'house-ruler', often used to signify the 'ruler of the nativity'. Here it corresponds to the "giver of years."

cause of the slowness of their motion. And when those three are conjoined in the same terms or face[1]; and the Sun aspects them, they will signify the destruction of sects and of kingdoms, and their change, and [other] great things according to the quantity of their strength and their rulership of their signs. And this is their greatest conjunction that signifies prophecy, and the destruction of some climes, and great things; and especially if any one of the inferior Planets helps them.

And you should know that the one that is stronger than the rest will be the significator. But if it is a benefic, it will signify good fortune; and if it is a malefic, it will signify evil and distress. Understand also that if these Planets are conjoined in their own exaltations, they will signify good and advantage at that time, and a multitude of excitements of wars, and the demonstration of miracles. But if they were conjoined in their own domiciles, they will signify detriment and dryness and barrenness of the land and famine, unless they are made fortunate.

And you will know that when they are joined together in a fire sign, they will also signify the barrenness of the land; and in a water sign, a multitude of rain. Also, in air signs they will signify the strength of the winds; and in earth signs, an excess of cold and of detriment. And when they are conjoined in masculine signs, they will signify a detriment to masculine animals; and in feminine signs, a detriment to feminine ones.

Chapter 10. *The Major Conjunction.*

Mâshâ'allâh said, we have already said that principal things happen from a Major Conjunction, which is a conjunction of the superior planets. But there are other conjunctions of these superior Planets that are also signifying major accidents. For the conjunction of Saturn and Jupiter is a greatest conjunction; and it signifies accidents and sects.

Moreover, the knowledge of the accidents resulting from it is

---

[1]Face = Decan.

had by looking at the ASC's and the planets at the hour of their conjunctions, and which one of them rules in the figure. And if it is a benefic, it will signify good and advantageous conditions for the time; but if it is a malefic, it will signify detriment and dryness, as well as barrenness of the land, and wars. Know therefore that when Jupiter is stronger than Saturn, it will signify good from that same conjunction. But if Saturn is the ruler, it will signify detriment and distress.

And know that their conjunction in fire signs and air signs will signify dryness and barrenness of the land, as well as heaviness[1] in the market, and the destruction of seeds in the lands, and famine. But in water signs, it will signify an excess of rains and pestilence, of such a condition that they are beset with difficulties. And finally, if they are benefics, they will signify an increase of good things in all the things that they signify, and a decrease in evil.

Also, you should know that when a major conjunction is in any one of the angles, and especially in the MC angle, it will signify the appearance of a king or a prophet from the part [of the World ruled by] the same sign. Moreover, if that same sign is fortunate and its ruler is good, it will signify his triumphs and domination; but if it is impedited and its ruler [too], it will signify his demise and downfall; and it will be a conjunction to be feared after the known years of that same conjunction, which we have mentioned elsewhere.

Chapter 11. *The Middling Conjunction.*

Mâshâ'allâh said, a Middling Conjunction is a conjunction of Mars and Saturn. And this signifies the occurrences of battles and the contrarieties of wars. And when you want to know about these same occurrences, know the dominating [Planet] in the figure of their conjunction; which, if it is a benefic, it will signify good and advantageous conditions; and if it is a malefic, it signifies evil and its impediment.

You should also know that their conjunction in human signs

---

[1]That is, low prices.

will signify a multitude of illnesses among them; and their conjunction in any one of the angles of [the Revolution of] the Year will signify contrarieties affecting rich persons or Kings and a multitude of wars; and that thing will last until they are joined to others in turn. And their conjunction in fire signs signifies dryness and barrenness of the land; and in air signs, winds; but in water signs a multitude of rains; and in earth signs, cold and snow and a multitude of cold. You should also know that when the benefics are in aspect, they will reduce the evil, and the malefics will increase it.

Test what I have said to you, and you will find it [valid], if God wills it!

Chapter 12. *The Minor Conjunction.*

Mâshâ'allâh said, a Minor Conjunction is a conjunction of Jupiter and Mars; and that signifies occurrences that are made by rains and snows, and corruption of the air, and war. But if a benefic wins the rulership of their conjunction, it will signify good fortune; and if a malefic wins, it will signify evil. And know that when Jupiter and Mars are conjoined in the ASC of the [Revolution of] the Year or in any one of its angles, it will signify unrest and diversity for kings, unless benefics are in aspect.

Know too that whenever a benefic is joined with a malefic, there will appear [something of] the nature of the stronger one of them. And when a malefic is joined to [another] malefic, evil will overflow, unless the Planet that rules the conjunction is a benefic.

Understand [now] that this is the last [chapter] that we have set forth in this book; and that it is from the secrets of the science of the stars!

Completed is the Book of Mâshâ'allâh translated by John of Seville in Luna from Arabic into Latin with the praise of God and His aid.

INDEX OF PERSONS

BIBLIOGRAPHY

al-Nadîm
The Fihrist of al-Nadîm.
edited and translated by Bayard Dodge
New York and London: Columbia University Press, 1970. 2
vols.

MÂSHÂ·ALLÂH

THE BOOK OF THOUGHTS
with
A NOTE ON INTERPRETATION

Translated from the Twelfth Century Latin Version
of John of Seville

by

JAMES HERSCHEL HOLDEN, M.A.
Fellow of the American Federation of Astrologers

Contents

Translator's Preface

Mâshâʾallâh was the adopted Muslim name of the Jewish astrologer Mîshâ ibn Athrâ from Basra, Iraq, who converted to Islam and became one of the greatest Arabian[1] astrologers. He was born about 730 A.D. and lived until about 815. He was one of the astrological consultants employed by the Caliph al-Manṣûr (679-777) to make an election for the founding of the new city of Baghdad in 762.[2] Al-Nadîm[3] says this about Mâshâʾallâh: "He was a man of distinction and during his period the leading person for the science of judgments of the stars."

He was probably acquainted with the Greek astrologer Theophilus (d. 777), who seems to have been the first prominent Arabian astrologer. Theophilus wrote several books on astrology that survive in Greek versions, but the Arabic versions were unknown to the Twelfth Century Translators, who turned much Arabian astrology into Latin and sparked the recovery of astrology in Western Europe. Hence, Theophilus is largely unknown to modern astrologers.

Mâshâʾallâh thus became the earliest Arabian astrologer whose works were known in the West. He wrote on a variety of subjects and was considered by both later Arabian astrologers and Euro-

---

[1] By *Arabian*, I mean all those, of whatever ethnic group, who wrote in the Arabic language.

[2] See my paper "The Foundation Chart of Baghdad" in *Today's Astrologer* Vol. 65, No. 3 (March 2, 2003): 9-10 & 29.

[3] From the priceless catalogue of Arabic literature as it existed at the end of the 10th century, *The Fihrist of al-Nadîm* edited and translated by Bayard Dodge (New York and London: Columbia University Press, 1970. 2 vols.), II, p. 650.

pean astrologers to be a prime authority. His *Book of Thoughts* is a short treatise on how to judge a Horary chart. In particular, how to determine the cause of the Question and its probable end.

Finally, Mâshâ'allâh states how an astrologer can misinterpret a Horary chart—either by getting the time wrong, or by trying to judge a poorly expressed Question, or by choosing the wrong significators.

The first edition of the Latin version of Mâshâ'allâh's book on the Significations of the Planets was published in 1493 by Bonetus Locatellus at Venice in an omnibus edition of astrological works. It was edited by Joachim Heller and reprinted by Montanus & Neuber in a nicer format at Nürnberg in 1549. I have used a copy of the Latin text included in that edition.

The Book of Thoughts

An *intention* results from *thoughts*; and Mâshâ'allâh directed that you should establish the ASC by its degree and minute; and the twelve houses most exactly.[1]

Moreover, there are three ways by which Questions are made. *First*, you should understand the cause about which he asks. *Second*, what cause impelled him [to ask it]. *Third*, you should know whether the thing can be perfected or not, and what end [result] is going to be had.

Therefore, when you want to know this, know the prime significator according to what I shall tell you. The knowledge of which, is that you should look at the ASC and its ruler, and the Moon and the ruler of its sign, and also the Sun and the ruler of its sign, and the ruler of the Hour, and the Part of Fortune.

And work with the one of them that has the most dignities and is in the better place. But if you do not find what I have just said to you, look at the ruler of the ASC, or the ruler of its exaltation, and the ruler of its terms, and the ruler of its triplicity, and the ruler of its face. And know which one of these is the one that is stronger in the ASC by the number of its own dignities, and look at it, and take that one to be the significator if it is in a good place. Besides, the goodness of a place [for a Planet] is when it is in some of its own dignities, or in a good place with respect to the Sun, or when it is in

---

[1]This seems to indicate that Mâshâ'allâh was using the either the Equal House or the Alchabitius system of House Division.

the angles free from the malefics.

Work therefore with the one that is stronger and has the most dignities and is in a better place. And know that the ruler of the ASC, when it is in the ASC, will be stronger than the others. But if it is not in the ASC, and the ruler of the exaltation of the ASC is in it, then it alone will be the significator and the more dignified. And so, the one that you will see is stronger in the circle because of its number of dignities, even if it is not in the ASC or in the other angles, and yet is stronger than the others in its sign, [that one will be the significator].

And know that the ruler of the ASC may be in the individual signs for two hours of efficacy over the many things of the Querent. But if the ruler of the ASC is the significator of all things, then all things of the Querent would be under that same sign, either good or evil, according to the signification of the ruler of the ASC, but it is not so!

Similarly too, the Moon may be joined to a particular Planet throughout the whole day, or for the greatest part of the day, and yet the significations of things are made to be diverse during that day, because some of them occur and others do not. Therefore, it is always necessary for us to seek out the [true] significator. Know therefore which one is the significator; and I say to you, [see] which one is selected with the ruler of the ASC namely and the Moon and the ruler of its sign by night. And also [look at] the Sun by day and the ruler of its sign; and also the planet that is in the angles—and especially in the ASC or in the MC—whichever one is stronger in its sign.

And know that an intention is truer that the Querent has had in his heart for one day and night or longer. When, therefore, you have found the significator, and you want to know the *cause* of the Question—that is, from what source the Question arose—look at which Planet the significator of the intention is separated from. And know that the *cause* of the Question is in accordance with the nature of the Planet from which the significator is separated.

And if you want to know the *end* of the intention, then know to which Planet the significator is joined; and know that the *end* of the intention will be according to the signification of the Planet to which it is joined.

And now I shall make an example for you, by which you will be able to perceive all Questions and the significations of all things, if God wills.

A Question was brought to us, whose ASC was the 10th degree of Taurus; and its ruler Venus was in Cancer in the 15th degree of the Moon's domicile; and the Moon similarly is in Libra, the domicile of Venus, in the 10th degree. And the Moon was peregrine because it was not in its own domicile, nor in its own exaltation, nor in its triplicity; but it was joined to Venus by a square aspect, and it was received by Venus. Also, the ruler of the Part of Fortune was Saturn, which was peregrine in Leo and not received.[1]

I looked therefore at all the Planets, but I did not find any one among them stronger than Venus, because it was the ruler of the ASC, and it was in its own triplicity. And so I looked at the sign in which it was, and it was in the domicile of the Moon. Then I began to look for the significator of Venus's sign—because Venus was the ruler of the ASC—and I found it in Libra, in the 5th house from the ASC,[2] and in the 4th house from the significator, which was Venus. And because the Moon signifies mothers, I knew by that that he is wanting to ask about his mother's illness, and he wants to know about her condition.

Therefore, I looked to see which Planet the Moon was separated

---

[1] Assuming that this was an actual Question (and not a hypothetical example), the time of the Question would have been when Saturn was in early Leo, viz. 770-771 A.D. or 799-800 A.D. But since the positions of no other planets are given, it is not possible to assign a definite date to the chart. However, a chart set for 28 May 771 at about 3:15 A.M. has the Planets in the right signs (although Saturn is in the 2nd face rather than the 1st). Another possible date is 24 Jun 801 at 1:45 A.M., but then Saturn was at the end of Leo rather than at the beginning. And both of these early times seem unlikely for a Question to be put in the 8th century.

[2] If Mâshâʾallâh was using Equal House house division, Venus would have been in the 5th house.

from, and it was separated from Saturn. Therefore I knew that she would be suffering from a cold and dry illness. And I wanted to know in what member [of the body] the illness would be located. And I looked at Saturn from the sign in which it was; and Saturn was in the first face of Leo; and of the members of the body, Leo has the stomach; and I said that it would appear in the stomach.

Moreover, since I would like to know what *end* the illness was going to have, I looked to see what Planet the Moon was joined to—i.e. which planet was signifying the intention—and it was being joined to Venus. And I said that she would be freed from the illness on account of Venus, which is a benefic and was receiving the Moon. And when I wanted to know the time of her recovery, I looked at the degrees of the configuration that was between Venus and the Moon, and I said that she would be recovered after as many days as there were degrees; and therefore I put the number of days at five, because the Moon was in a mobile sign. If it had been in a common sign, you would put months [instead]; and if it would have been in a fixed sign, you would put years. And if the Moon would have been joined to Saturn or Mars, I would have said that she would die after that length of time.

And so, look at the *intention*, at what is hidden, and in all things about which you are asked; for in that way you may know what the end will be. And similarly, reckon the time of the performance of all things according to this example. And combine the signification of the planets with the signification of the signs, and the thing of every intention and every Question will be plain to you, according to what I have set forth for you, if God wills.

And know that if Venus would have been in the place of the Moon, I would have said that he is asking about a woman. And moreover, if Venus would have been in the 7th, I would have said that he is asking about his wife; and if it would have been in the 5th, about his children; and in the 11th, about his friends. And if the Sun would have been in the place of the Moon, I would have said that he is asking about his father; and if it would have been in the 10th, about the king. And if it would have been in the ASC, about some rulership; in the 9th, about faith; in the 3rd, about travel.

And if Mars would have been in the place of the Moon, he is asking about a fugitive or about an armed robber. And if it would have been in the ASC, it would have signified fear; if in the 2nd, robbery and the taking way of things. And in the 3rd, his brother; in the 5th, an adversary or a pregnant woman. And if Mercury would have been in the place of Venus, he would have asked about a letter, or about knowledge. And if Jupiter would have been in the 9th, it would be said that he would have been asking about a dream.

And truly I have now explained to you how you should combine the significations of the Planets.

ON INTERPRETATION

Know that an Astrologer can err in four ways. *First*, when his astrolabe is false, or if he takes the shadow in an uneven place or in a crooked line.[1] *Second*, when the Querent does not know how to pose his Question. *Third*, when he has asked, and it will not be certain whether the Sun is already in the MC or not.[2] *Fourth*, when the benefics and the malefics are equal in strength, for the astrologer can err or be deceived in the strength of the benefics and the malefics.

Moreover, in every Question that is free from difficulties of this sort, if you know the significator rightly, you will be able to judge truly, and you will not err. And you should not work by estimation, that is do not make an arbitrary judgment without any reason [to support it], because if you do, you will rarely find the truth.

---

[1] In the old days, before clocks, the astrologer was obliged to find the time of day from an instrument such as an astrolabe or a sundial. And if he had a bad astrolabe or if his sundial was not level or properly oriented, he would obtain the wrong time.

[2] It is difficult to judge by eye whether the Sun is a few degrees to the east of the MC or to the west.